THE
NEW AGE
CULT

THE NEW AGE CULT

Walter Martin, Ph.D.

Founder and Director of
Christian Research Institute International
Irvine, California

with
The Research Staff of CRI

Elliot Miller, M.A.
Ron Rhodes, Th.D.
Dan Schlesinger, M.A.

BETHANY HOUSE PUBLISHERS
MINNEAPOLIS, MINNESOTA 55438
A Division of Bethany Fellowship, Inc.

Published by Bethany House Publishers
A Division of Bethany Fellowship, Inc.
6820 Auto Club Road, Minneapolis, Minnesota 55438

Printed in the United States of America

Library of Congress Cataloging-in-Publication Data

Martin, Walter Ralston, 1928–
    The New Age cult.

    Bibliography: p.
    Includes index.
    1. New Age movement—Controversial literature.
2. Occultism—Religious aspects—Christianity.
I. Christian Research Institute. II. Title.
BP605.N48M365   1989   299'.93   89–6889
ISBN 1–55661–077–7

For Darlene, my wife,
who never lets me forget my deadlines and whose love and
support is a constant source of inspiration.

WALTER MARTIN holds four earned degrees, having received his doctorate from California Coast University in the field of Comparative Religions. Author of a dozen books and a half-dozen booklets and many articles, he is nationally known as "The Bible Answer Man," host of a popular syndicated radio call-in program which is heard across the country. He is founder and director of the Christian Research Institute, located in Irvine, California.

Preface

This is a very difficult book to write, not because the subject is unimportant—it is terribly important—but because so many people, Christian and non-Christian alike, know so little about the evils of New Age thinking.

It is also difficult because almost 35 years ago I warned of the New Age movement and correctly predicted the growth of the occult. I wish I had been wrong! I wrote articles and chapters in books on the cults of Theosophy, the Unity School of Christianity, Christian Science, Spiritism, Bahaiism, and Rosicrucianism, all of which were spearheads of current New Age teachings.

As Founder and Director of Zondervan Publishing House's division of Cult Apologetics from 1955–65, and founder and director of Christian Research Institute since 1960, I urged Christian publishers to commission and distribute books, booklets, pamphlets, and tracts on these cults and the occult, which were even then a growing threat to the Church. I have delivered thousands of lectures, crisscrossing America and the world for over 38 years trying to get the message across. Sometimes I felt like a frustrated Paul Revere calling out *"The cults are coming, the cults are coming!"* which I'm sure sounded to many like a litany of impending disaster. But so it has proved to be.

Today some 35 to 50 million people are involved in some form of cultic organization throughout America and on foreign mission fields. Almost 60 million dabble in some New Age practice or occultic thinking. Over the last 25 years, national magazines, newspapers, and radio and television programs have proclaimed and trumpeted the New Age cult.

Time magazine has featured the New Age movement (or the world of the occult) in two cover stories, one showing Shirley MacLaine and the other, a masked high priest of the church of Satan.

The dusty old occult bookstores and virtually unknown publishers have given way to well advertised sections in B. Dalton, Walden Books, Doubleday, Brentano's, Crown, and other major stores and distributors. The *American Bookseller* did a full issue on New Age publications in January 1988, and *Time* noted that more than 2,500 New Age or occultic bookstores now exist in the United States alone. Obscure names and titles such as Alice Baily, Madame Helena Blavatsky, Annie Besant, Moses Hull, the Secret Doctrine, The Plan, Anthroposophy, and the Lucis Trust are familiar in the mass media, even admired in some cases and revered by New Age adherents.

During the late 1950s and into the mid–1960s, the New Age movement—or *cult*, as it is properly designated—was like a great iceberg, nine-tenths below the surface. However in the 1960s it began to grow bold, surfacing in full force by the 1980s. The Church by and large did not respond to it until the iceberg had surfaced, and even then we only half heartedly attacked the problem.

We have had enough of "just be positive and preach the gospel" or "don't offend people by defending your Christian faith or criticizing false teachings; God will protect the church." There can be little doubt that in the wake of the New Age holocaust, the time for action is *now* and we must be prepared to "give an answer to every man that asketh you of the hope that is in you" (1 Peter 3:15).

Throughout history, every time the Church has failed to do this, false doctrines and heretical teachings have plagued us. Only the Church militant can become the Church triumphant. The challenge is here, the time is now! By divine grace we still have time to confront and evangelize those in the New Age Cult. The cult is the world of occultic darkness and spiritual danger beyond belief.

This small volume is obviously not intended to replace a select number of good, in-depth studies of the New Age movement (see my recommended list at the back of this book), but it is theology in newspaper language, a popular layman's overview and refutation of a militant and growing problem for Christians everywhere.

May our Lord be pleased to use it to re-echo the warnings given more than three decades ago and inspire Christians to both the proclamation and defense of "the faith that was once for all entrusted to the saints" (Jude 3, NIV).

Walter Martin
San Juan Capistrano,
California
March 1989

OTHER BOOKS BY WALTER MARTIN . . .

BOOKLETS

Contents

Acknowledgments

I wish to thank Elliot Miller, editor of the *Christian Research Journal*; Ron Rhodes, his assistant; Dan Schlesinger, Research Coordinator at Christian Research Institute; Craig Hawkins; and, those of our staff who assisted in the preparation and editing of this volume.

Their dedication to excellence in detail and in Christian apologetics, particularly in the realm of New Age research has contributed greatly to this effort. Special thanks to Oona Fritz for her patience and diligent pursuit of all the details of publishing this work.

Chapter 1

The World of the Occult and the New Age

The turbulent sixties provided the perfect atmosphere for what we now recognize as the New Age movement or the New Age Cult. The neoorthodox theologian Nels Ferre correctly predicted the influx of Eastern and Indian philosophy and theology that characterized that decade, and concluded that the imported ideas would be a major challenge to historic Christianity.

The great English apologist and writer C. S. Lewis saw the battle lines clearly drawn. He noted that in the final conflict between religions, Hinduism and Christianity would offer the only viable options because Hinduism absorbs all religious systems, and Christianity excludes all others, maintaining the supremacy of the claims of Jesus Christ.

New Age Roots

To understand the New Age movement, it is necessary that we recognize its ancient roots in the occult. The word *occult* comes from the Latin word for secret and mysterious.

The Bible forbids occultic practices, stating that they draw on satanic power.

The Bible describes several different dimensions or realms of reality such as heaven, hell, and the visible universe. But yet another dimension commands our attention. In Ephesians 2 and 6, the Apostle Paul speaks of this dimension as the realm of "the prince of the power of the air, the spirit that now worketh in the children of disobedience" (Eph. 2:2). He declares that the Christian is engaged in spiritual combat against the forces that dominate that realm. In Paul's words, "our struggle is not against flesh and blood, but against the rulers, against the authorities, against the powers of this dark world and against the spiritual forces of evil in the heavenly realms" (Eph. 6:12, NIV). The apostle goes to great lengths in his writings to warn us against "the devil's schemes" (Eph. 6:11, NIV), echoing the words of Moses to the Israelites in the Old Testament. Moses communicated God's extreme displeasure with the inhabitants of the land of Canaan, who practiced abominable things and were, in effect, Satan worshipers:

> When you enter the land the Lord your God is giving you, do not learn to imitate the detestable ways of the nations there. Let no one be found among you who sacrifices his son or daughter in the fire, who practices divination or sorcery, interprets omens, engages in witchcraft, or casts spells, or who is a medium or spiritist or who consults the dead. Anyone who does these things is detestable to the Lord, and because of these detestable practices the Lord your God will drive out those nations before you. You must be blameless before the Lord your God. The nations you will dispossess listen to those who practice sorcery or divination. But as for you, the Lord your God has not permitted you to do so. (Deut. 18:9–14, NIV)

This veritable glossary of the occult warned Israel of impending wrath if they followed in the footsteps of the inhabitants of the land that God had chosen to give them.

The occult might be called a substitute faith that is found

throughout the history of world religions—including the Hebrews themselves, as seen in their esoteric and occultic book *The Kabala*. The Bible speaks repeatedly against all occultic practices, giving special attention to astrologers (Isa. 47) and those who were called "sorcerers" or "magicians," as recorded in the book of Daniel.

There can be little doubt after reading 2 Kings 21 that God's judgment did come upon Israel for her failure to obey His commands concerning the occult. King Manassah violated all the prohibitions against the occult, bringing about the exile of the Jews, which eventually led to their repentance and restoration.

The New Age Cult is a revival of this ancient occultism. It holds historical ties to Sumerian, Indian, Egyptian, Chaldean, Babylonian, and Persian religious practices.

The term "New Age movement" or "New Age Cult" is a fresh title, but, as *Time* magazine pointed out, the occult is nothing new: "So here we are in the New Age, a combination of spirituality and superstition, fad and farce, about which the only thing certain is that it is not new."[1]

The Theosophical Connection

For all practical purposes, the New Age Cult can be equated with the transplantation of Hindu philosophy through the Theosophical Society founded by Helena Blavatsky in the latter part of the nineteenth century in the United States. Madame Blavatsky, as she was known, promoted spiritism, seances, and basic Hindu philosophy while manifesting a distinct antagonism to biblical Christianity.

Marilyn Ferguson, in her book *The Aquarian Conspiracy*, notes that the "Age of Aquarius" occupies a center seat in the arena of New Age thinking, and when coupled with the emphasis of such cults as Christian Science, New Thought, the Unity School of Christianity, Rosicrucianism, and Science of Mind, or Religious Science, it becomes a formidable vehicle for New Age thinking.

---

[1]*Time* magazine, Dec. 7, 1987, p. 62.

The theology of the New Age movement assumes an evolutionary process. The world is waiting for more revealers of truth (*avatars*), such as Buddha, Mohammed, Confucius, Zoroaster, Moses, Krishna, and ultimately one designated as the Lord Maitreya, an incarnation of the Buddha, the Enlightened One. The Lord Jesus Christ is relegated to the role of a demi-god or "one of many equally good ways." He's most surely not *the* way, *the* truth, and *the* life, as He taught in John 14:6.

A tremendously significant figure in the history of the development of the New Age thinking is Alice Bailey, who was involved with Madame Blavatsky in the Theosophical Society. She wrote more than 20 books, allegedly influenced by a spirit guide who communicated with her telepathically. Elliot Miller, writing in the Summer 1987 *Christian Research Journal*, made this observation:

> In Bailey's *The Externalization of the Hierarchy*, the same book in which the year 1975 is given significance in the Hierarchy's plan, we are also told that "in 2025 the date in all probability will be set for the first stage of the externalization [bodily appearances] of the Hierarchy" (p. 530). Later on we are told that after these first masters appear "if these steps prove successful, other and more important reappearances will be possible, beginning with the return of Christ" (p. 559).

Miller correctly points out that if Bailey's disciples are following her plan, and if Bailey is right about the significance of the year 1975, then the "christ" cannot appear until some time after 2025. In context, 1975 represents only a beginning, a stepping up of preparatory activity for a 50-year period.

In *Problems of Humanity* by Alice Bailey, we also find another interesting observation relative to the event that is called "the festival of humanity":

> [The festival of humanity] will be preeminently [the day] on which the divine nature of man will be recognized and his power to express goodwill and establish human rights relations [because of his divinity] will

be stressed. On this festival we are told Christ has for nearly 2,000 years represented humanity and has stood before the Hierarchy as the god-man, the leader of his people and the eldest in the great family of brothers" (p. 164).

Important as Alice Bailey's writings are, they obviously cannot be held as an infallible guide for New Age evolution.

But the Theosophical Society did fuel the emerging New Age movement, and through the activities of Madame Blavatsky and Annie Besant, the society planned for the Lord Maitreya to appear in the person of Mrs. Besant's protege, Krishna murti. However, Krishna murti declined the honor of Mrs. Besant's anointing due largely to the death of his brother and his subsequent disillusionment with the claims of Theosophy. And so the search and the anticipation continued.

The Christ of the New Age

In 1982, newspapers across the country displayed full-page advertisements boldly stating: "The world has had enough . . . of hunger, injustice, and war. There is an answer to our call for help, a world teacher for all humanity. THE CHRIST IS NOW HERE."

This was sponsored by the Tara Foundation under the leadership of Benjamin Creme, and asked such interesting questions as *Who Is the Christ?*, *What Is He Saying?*, and *When Will We See Him?* The ad ended in a call for peace: "Without sharing there can be no justice, without justice there can be no peace, without peace there can be no future."

Three other New Age groups joined the Tara Foundation, but the nebulous ad inevitably failed to attract the kind of attention Creme had anticipated. The "christ" of whom the Tara Foundation was speaking was not the Christ of biblical revelation, but an Indian guru who had flown to England (thus fulfilling Rev. 1:7), and now lives in London. Mr. Creme stated that this christ would meet the press, but the press conference was later postponed.

Mr. Creme, in his book *The Reappearance of the Christ*, ran true to New Age thought when describing the relationship of Jesus Christ to the New Age:

> The christ is not God, he is not coming as God. He is an embodiment of an aspect of God, the love aspect of God. He is the embodied soul of all creation. He embodies the energy which is a consciousness aspect of the Being we call God. . . . He would rather that you didn't pray to him, but to God within you, which is also within him. . . . He said it himself. "The kingdom of God is within you" (p. 135).

Such statements from New Age leaders characterize the movement as pointedly anti-Christian and particularly hostile to the unique claim of deity by the Lord Jesus Christ and confirmed by apostolic witness. In a fact sheet released by the Christian Research Institute dealing with the New Age movement, a report with which I concur, the New Age movement has been described as:

> The most common name used to portray the growing penetration of Eastern and occultic mysticism into Western culture. The words *New Age* refer to the Aquarian Age, which occultists believe to be dawning, bringing with it an era of enlightenment and peace. Encompassed within the New Age movement are various cults which emphasize a mystic experience (including Transcendental Meditation, the Rajneesh cult, Eckankar, the Church Universal and Triumphant, the Divine Light Mission, and many others). The followers of various gurus, such as the late swami Muktananda, Sai Baba, Baba Ram Dass, Mahareeshi Mahesh Yoga, and Guru Maharijih, personify the essence of modern New Age leadership. Other groups such as the "Human Potential Movement" exemplified in Est (or The Forum), Lifespring, Silva Mind Control, Summit Workshops, etc., and many (though not all) of the advocates of the various approaches to holistic health, accurately represent the spirit of the New Age.

Though the beliefs and emphases of the various groups

and individuals who make up the New Age movement can vary widely, they share a common religious experience and philosophical base. The theological similarity in the midst of diversity is much like the many traditions within historic Christianity that differ on peripheral doctrines and yet share a common experience with the Holy Spirit resulting from a common faith in Jesus Christ. Members of the New Age movement share a common belief that "all is one," that is, everything that exists together composes one essential reality or substance. This ultimate reality is identified as God, usually seen as an impersonal consciousness and power.

The Divinity of All Mankind

The New Age derives its belief in the inherent divinity of man from this belief in the divinity of all things. Thus the separation of the human race from God which is obvious to the Christian Church is treated differently by the New Age movement. Whereas historic Christianity believes that man was separated from God by his transgression of God's law, the New Age movement believes that man is separated from God *only* in his own consciousness. He is the victim of a false sense of separate identity that blinds him to his essential unity with God.

Thus the New Age movement advocates various methods of altering the consciousness (Yoga, meditation, chanting, ecstatic dancing, drugs, etc.) as the means of salvation. These enable man to consciously experience his supposed union with God, an experience defined as "enlightenment."

The New Age Cult also heavily emphasizes the ancient Hindu doctrines of *reincarnation* and *karma*. The law of karma teaches that whatever a person does, good or bad, will return to him in *exact* proportion in another existence. Since most people are not able to pay off in one lifetime all of the bad karma that they have accumulated for their bad deeds, they are compelled to return in new incarnations until all of their bad karma has been balanced by the good karma they achieve.

The New Age Conspiracy

We can state that the Aquarian Conspiracy, which the New Age writer Marilyn Ferguson describes in her book by that title, actually exists. Many people within the overall New Age movement believe that they can hasten the coming of the age of peace by working together to influence developments in Western culture's political, economic, educational, and religious life.

Among some of these people there are definite efforts underway to promote the development of a united worldwide society. However, we have not found anything to substantiate claims that everyone involved in the New Age movement is a part of this conspiracy. (Many of the New Age cults are exclusive, so it is difficult to imagine them working to enthrone any world ruler beside their own particular leaders.) Nor have we yet found evidence that any specific individual has been selected to occupy the place of world ruler. We have not seen evidence to show that the conspiracy is so highly developed and influential that it is presently in a position to accomplish its goal of a one-world culture.

However, the New Age movement could certainly play a part in the great deception of the tribulation described in various biblical prophecies, and we should definitely keep it under observation. But it would be counterproductive for the body of Christ to respond to this movement with hysteria over a public declaration that the New Age movement is involved in conscious conspiratorial activities that cannot be factually substantiated.

The New Age movement's efforts to infiltrate our society with Eastern mysticism must be resisted, and their activities must be monitored, but it must be done in a sane, biblical manner, in a spirit of "peaceful sobriety."

The rise of the New Age Cult over the last quarter of a century should be a sobering reminder to the Christian Church that we cannot rest upon the laurels of past evangelism and pioneer missionary activities. The old maxim is true: "The price of liberty is eternal vigilance."

The Importance of the New Age Movement

In the *Time* article already alluded to, *Time* states that "a strange mix of spirituality and superstition is sweeping across the country, and this is mirrored in the renewal of interest in the world of occultism." *Time* pointed out that Bantam Books, one of the largest publishers of paperbacks in the United States, "says its New Age titles have increased tenfold in the past decade. The number of New Age bookstores has doubled in the past five years to about 2,500 . . . and fledgling magazines with names like *New Age, Body, Mind, & Spirit*, and *Brain-Mind Bulletin*" have made their appearance upon the religious scene. According to Dr. John Weldon and John Ankerberg in their illuminating article "The Facts on the New Age movement," "more than 3,000 publishers of occult books and journals" along with the sales of New Age books have turned interest in the New Age into a "one-billion-dollar-a-year business."

The New Age movement is not important just because it has a multi-billion dollar balance sheet, but because it reaches out to multiple millions who are dazzled by celebrities such as Shirley MacLaine, Merv Griffin, Linda Evans, John Denver, Phalicia Rashad, and Sharon Gless, who all say their concept of reality and religious truth works.

Shirley MacLaine is a prime example of this. In her book *Out on a Limb*, she promotes New Age thinking. She sponsors seminars that to date have raised 3 million dollars to build the New Age showcase center in Baca, Colorado, between 1989–90. It is virtually impossible to turn on talk shows—radio or TV—that do not feature some New Age psychic, astrologer, or guru with the latest word on "spiritual reality."

The Threat of the New Age Cult

The New Age movement is penetrating our educational system as well as some of our state legislatures. We are told that even Nancy Reagan, wife of the former President of the United States, consults an astrologer, especially after the assassination attempt on her husband confirmed an astrologer's warning of imminent danger.

The New Age movement threatens not only the foundation of the Judeo-Christian religion, but challenges fundamental belief in the existence of objective truth. In New Age thinking, truth is perceived *individually*, and it is not uncommon for the New Age believer to say "that's your truth, this is mine," as if truth like beauty exists only in the eye of the beholder. The threat of the New Age movement cannot be underestimated in our public schools where children are taught *mantras*, meditation words, and meditation techniques. They are subjected to "values clarification" in which moral, ethical, and spiritual values become purely subjective in nature and not subject to any meanings apart from those assigned by the child. In this jumbled scenario, reality becomes lost in a shuffle of conflicting vocabulary and the law of the semantic jungle declares pragmatism: "If it works, use it—if it feels good, do it."

It is no wonder that *Time*, quoting several Christian writers, noted:

> Humans are essentially religious creatures and they don't rest until they have some sort of answers to the fundamental questions. Rationalism and secularism don't answer those questions. But you can see the rise of the New Age is a barometer of the disintegration of American culture. Dostoyevsky said [that] anything is permissible if there is no God. But anything is also permissible if everything is God. There is no way to make any distinction between good and evil . . . once you've deified yourself, which is what the New Age is all about, there is no higher moral absolute. It's a recipe for ethical anarchy . . . it's both messianic and millennial."[2]

Sacrificing Biblical Revelation

The deification of man by the New Age Cult requires the abandonment of absolute truth, worship at the altar of relativism, and obsession with reincarnation. The cult is a grow-

---

[2]*Time*, Dec. 7, 1987, p. 72.

ing threat to Christians and to those who take seriously biblical admonitions such as "I have made the earth . . . even my hands have stretched out the heavens. . . . Thou shalt love the Lord thy God with all thy heart, and with all thy soul, and with all thy mind. . . . Thou shalt love thy neighbor as thyself. On these two commandments hang all the law and the prophets" (Isa. 45:12; Matt. 22:37–40).

The New Age movement embraces what has been termed "monistic pantheism," all is one and all is God. Since the movement believes man is divine just as Satan once promised he would be in Eden (Gen. 3:5), the next great event is the dawn of the millennial kingdom. In the Aquarian era, peace, prosperity, love, and satisfaction are all within the grasp of those who are willing to exchange biblical revelation for Hindu speculation and the Prince of Life for the Prince of Darkness.

There can be little doubt that the Aquarian Conspiracy, the rise of the New Age Cult, and the Bible have one common denominator. The Bible prophesies that at the end of the ages, false prophets, christs, and teachers will proliferate (Matt. 24), proclaiming "here is Christ, there he is" (Luke 21). In the words of the living Christ, "This day is the scripture fulfilled in your ears" (Luke 4:21).

Chapter 2

Ten Key Doctrines of the New Age Movement

We often find ourselves reading someone's interpretation of what the leaders of the New Age movement say. In this chapter we will look at ten key doctrines and present, without interpretation, what New Age writers have said.

1. God

The late Jane Roberts was used to channel a disembodied entity named Seth. This is a thumbnail sketch of Seth's concept of God:

"He is not one individual, but an energy gestalt . . . a psychic pyramid of interrelated, ever-expanding consciousness that creates, simultaneously and instantaneously, universes and individuals that are given—through the gift of personal perspective—duration, psychic comprehension, intelligence, and eternal validity.

"This absolute, every-expanding, instantaneous psychic gestalt, which you may call God if you prefer, is so secure in its existence that it can constantly break itself down and rebuild itself.

"Its energy is so unbelievable that it does indeed form all universes; and because its energy is within and behind all universes, systems, and fields, it is indeed aware of each sparrow that falls, for it *is* each sparrow that falls."[1]

"In a sense there is no such thing as God, God does not exist. And in another sense, there is nothing else but God— only God exists. . . . All is God. And because all is God, there is no God."[2]

2. The Trinity

"Eternal Thought is one; in essence it is two—Intelligence and Force; and when they breathe, a child is born; this child is Love.

"And thus the Triune God stands forth, whom men call Father-Mother-Child."[3]

3. Jesus Christ

"People have been led to leave the churches in large numbers because the churches have presented a picture of the Christ impossible for the majority of thinking people today to accept—as the one and only Son of God, sacrificed by His Loving Father to save Humanity from the results of its sins; as a Blood Sacrifice straight out of the old and outworn Jewish Dispensation; as the unique revealer of God's nature, once and forever, never to be enlarged and expanded as man himself grows in awareness and ability to receive other revelations of that Divine nature; and as waiting in some mythical and unattractive Heaven until the end of the world, when He will return in a cloud of glory to the sound of Angels' trumpets, and descending from these clouds, inherit His Kingdom.

"The majority of thinking people today have rejected this view. . . ."[4]

[1]Jane Roberts, *The Seth Material* (Englewood Cliffs, N.J.: Prentice-Hall, 1970), pp. 237–38.
[2]Benjamin Creme, *The Reappearance of the Christ and the Masters of Wisdom* (London: The Tara Press, 1980), p. 110.
[3]Levi, *The Aquarian Gospel of Jesus the Christ* (Santa Monica, Calif.: DeVorss & Co., 1907), p. 100.
[4]Creme, *The Reappearance of Christ*, p. 25.

"What is the Christ? Within all life there exists a quality, an energy, which has as its basic characteristic irresistible growth, irresistible and inevitable expression of divinity. It is a quality which says that whatever form I am enclosed in, I will not be held a prisoner by that form, but I will transform it into a greater form. I will use all life, all experiences as stepping stones to greater revelations of divinity. The Christ is the basic evolutionary force within creation."[5]

"The true birth of the Christ was not the birth of Jesus. Jesus was an individual who himself had to recapitulate certain stages. He built upon the pattern the Buddha had established. . . . He himself had to become awakened. He had to, in his consciousness, touch this Christ pattern."[6]

"Jesus was an ideal Jew, born in Bethlehem of Judea. His mother was a beautiful Jewish girl named Mary. As a child Jesus differed but little from other children only that in past lives he had overcome carnal propensities to such an extent that he could be tempted like others and not yield. . . .

"In many respects Jesus was a remarkable child, for by ages of strenuous preparation he was qualified to be an avatar, a saviour of the world, and from childhood he was endowed with superior wisdom and was conscious of the fact that he was competent to lead the raid into the higher ways of spiritual living. . . .

"Edward was not always king, and Lincoln was not always president, and Jesus was not always Christ. Jesus won his Christship by a strenuous life."[7]

"Jesus: 'Men call me Christ, and God has recognized the name; but Christ is not a man. The Christ is universal Love and Love is King. . . .

" 'This Jesus is but man who has been fitted by temptations overcome, by trials multiform, to be the temple through which the Christ can manifest to men. . . .

" 'Then hear, you men of Israel, hear! Look not upon the flesh (i.e., the person of Jesus); it is not king. Look to the

[5]David Spangler, *Reflections on the Christ* (Moray, Scotland: Findhorn Publications, 1978), p. 13.
[6]Spangler, *Reflections*, p. 6.
[7]Levi, *The Aquarian Gospel*, pp. 13–14.

Christ within who shall be formed in every one of you, as he is formed in me.' "[8]

"Jesus: 'You know that all my life was one great drama for the sons of men; a pattern for the sons of men. I live to show the possibilities of man.

" 'What I have done all men can do, and what I am, all men shall be.' "[9]

"Jesus (claimed to be communicating through the late trance-channel Helen Schucman: 'Equals should not be in awe of one another because awe implies inequality. It is therefore an inappropriate reaction to me. . . . There is nothing about me that you cannot attain. I have nothing that does not come from God. The difference between us now is that I have nothing else. This leaves me in a state which is only potential in you.

" 'No man cometh unto the Father but by me' does not mean that I am in any way separate or different from you except in time, and time does not exist."[10]

4. The Atonement

"Jesus: 'In milder forms a parent says, "This hurts me more than it hurts you," and feels exonerated in beating a child. Can you believe your Father really thinks this way? It is so essential that all such things be dispelled that we must be sure that nothing of this kind remains in your mind. I was not "punished" because you were bad. . . .

" 'God does not believe in retribution. His Mind does not create that way. He does not hold your "evil" deeds against you. Is it likely that He would hold them against me? . . .

" 'Sacrifice is a notion totally unknown to God. It arises solely from fear, and frightened people can be vicious. Sacrificing in any way is a violation of my injunction that you should be merciful even as your Father in Heaven is merciful.' "[11]

---

[8]Levi, *The Aquarian Gospel*, p. 14.
[9]Levi, *The Aquarian Gospel*, p. 265.
[10]*A Course in Miracles* (Foundation for Inner Peace, 1975), vol. 1, p. 5.
[11]Ibid., pp. 32–33.

"Jesus: 'The crucifixion is nothing more than an extreme example. Its value, like the value of any teaching device, lies solely in the kind of learning it facilitates. . . .

" 'The message the crucifixion was intended to teach was that it is not necessary to perceive any form of assault in persecution, because you cannot *be* persecuted (i.e., because you are "God's Son," and therefore indestructible). If you respond with anger, you must be equating yourself with the destructible, and are therefore regarding yourself insanely.' "[12]

"This is really the true crucifixion. It was not so much hanging Jesus on the physical cross, but it was the entry of the cosmic Christ in the physical, etheric, mental, and emotional energy patterns of the planetary body itself.

"From that point onward, the Christ was no longer an educative force standing outside the planet, beckoning evolution forward. It had become a very powerful force operative within the very structure of the planet itself."[13]

5. Salvation

"Jesus: 'The real world is achieved when you perceive the basis of forgiveness is quite real and fully justified [i.e., that as "God's Son" you are really sinless and thus *deserve* forgiveness]. While you regard it as a gift unwarranted, it must uphold the guilt you would "forgive." Unjustified forgiveness is attack [i.e., it "attacks" you by telling you that you are a sinner in spite of your forgiveness]. And this is all the world can ever give. It pardons "sinners" sometimes, but remains aware that they have sinned. And so they do not merit the forgiveness that it gives.

" 'This is the false forgiveness which the world employs to keep the sense of sin alive. And recognizing God is just, it seems impossible His pardon could be real. Thus we have a fear of God, the sure result of seeing pardon as unmerited. No one who sees himself as guilty can avoid the fear of God.' "[14]

---

[12]Ibid., pp. 84–85.
[13]Spangler, *Reflections*, p. 7.
[14]*Course*, p. 594.

"Jesus: 'How simple is salvation! All it says is what was never true (i.e., sin and its punishment) is not true now, and never will be. The impossible has not occurred, and can have no effects. And that is all.' "[15]

"Today the motive shifts from the concept of personal salvation (which is assumed or taken for granted), and the preparation required is that of working with strength and understanding to bring about right human relations—a broader objective. There we have a motive which is not self-centered but which ranges each individual worker and humanitarian on the side of the spiritual Hierarchy, putting him in touch with all men of goodwill."[16]

6. Heaven and Hell and the Last Judgment

"Christianity has emphasized immortality but has made eternal happiness dependent upon the acceptance of a theological dogma: Be a true professing Christian and live in a somewhat fatuous heaven or refuse to be an accepting Christian, or a negative professional Christian, and go to an impossible hell—a hell growing out of the theology of the Old Testament and its presentation of a God full of hate and jealousy. Both concepts are today repudiated by all sane, sincere, thinking people. No one of any true reasoning power or with any true belief in a God of love accepts the heaven of the churchmen or has any desire to go there. Still less do they accept the 'lake which burneth with fire and brimstone' (Rev. 21:8) or the everlasting torture to which a God of love is supposed to condemn all who do not believe in the theological interpretations of the Middle Ages, of the modern fundamentalists, or of the unreasoning churchmen who seek—through doctrine, fear, and threat—to keep people in line with the obsolete old teaching."[17]

"Jesus: 'My brother, man, your thoughts are wrong; your heaven is not far away; and it is not a place of metes and

---

[15] *Course*, p. 600.
[16] Alice A. Bailey, *The Reappearance of the Christ* (New York: Lucis Publishing Company, 1948), p. 171.
[17] Ibid., pp. 146–147.

bounds, is not a country to be reached; it is a state of mind.

" 'God never made a heaven for man; he never made a hell'; we are creators and we make our own."

" 'Now, cease to seek for heaven in the sky; just open up the windows of your heart, and, like a flood of light, a heaven will come and bring a boundless joy; then toil will be no cruel task.' "[18]

"Those who believe in a hell and assign themselves to it through their belief can indeed experience one, but certainly in nothing like eternal terms. No should is forever ignorant."[19]

"Jesus: 'The Last Judgment is one of the most threatening ideas in your thinking. This is because you do not understand it. Judgment is not an attribute of God. It was brought into being only after the separation (i.e., man's fall into delusion), when it became one of the many learning devices to be built into the overall plan. . . .

" 'The Last Judgment is generally thought of as a procedure undertaken by God. Actually it will be undertaken by my brothers with my help. It is a final healing rather than a meting out of punishment, however much you may think that punishment is deserved. Punishment is a concept totally opposed to right-mindedness, and the aim of the Last Judgment is to restore right-mindedness to you. The Last Judgment might be called a process of right evaluation. It simply means that everyone will finally come to understand what is worthy and what is not. After this, the ability to choose can be directed rationally.' "[20]

7. Demonic Powers

"It is important to see that Lucifer, as I am using this term, describes an angel, a being, a great and mighty planetary consciousness. It does not describe that popular thought-form of Satan who seeks to lead man down a path of sin and wrongdoing. That is a human creation, and yet it is a creation

---

[18]Levi, *The Aquarian Gospel*, p. 71.
[19]Jane Roberts, *Seth Speaks* (Englewood Cliffs, N.J.: Prentice-Hall, 1972), 282–83.
[20]*Course*, pp. 29–30.

that has some validity but represents the collective thought-form of all those negative energies which man has built up and created.

"Man is his own Satan just as man is his own salvation. But since the energies of Lucifer go to build up this thought-form, Lucifer, or shall I say a shadow Lucifer, can be identified with this thought-form and in this there is confusion. If one can approach this collective thought-form with love, without fear, then one can go beyond this shadow and see the true angel of light that is there seeking to bring light to man's inner world."[21]

"Of course, yes, the forces of evil are part of God. They are not separate from God. Everything is God."[22]

8. The Second Coming of Christ

"In a very real sense, Findhorn (a New Age community in Scotland) represents the Second Coming. Any individual, any center, who so embodies the new that it becomes a magnetic source to draw the new out of the rest of the world, embodies the Second Coming."[23]

"In the esoteric tradition, the Christ is not the name of an individual but of an Office in the Hierarchy. The present holder of that office, the Lord Maitreya, has held it for 2,600 years, and manifested in Palestine through His Disciple, Jesus, by the occult method of overshadowing, the most frequent form used for the manifestation of avatars. He has never left the work, but for 2,000 years has waited and planned for the immediate future time, training His disciples, and preparing himself for the awesome task which awaits Him. He has made it known that this time, He himself will come."[24]

9. Reincarnation

"If the goal of right human relations will be taught universally by the Christ, the emphasis of His teaching *must* be

---

[21]Spangler, *Reflections*, p. 39.
[22]Creme, *The Reappearance of Christ*, p. 103.
[23]Spangler, *Reflections*, p. 10.
[24]Creme, *The Reappearance of Christ*, p. 30.

laid upon the Law of Rebirth. This is inevitably so, because in the recognition of this law will be found the solution of all the problems of humanity, and the answer to much of human questioning.

"This doctrine will be one of the keynotes of the new world religion, as well as the clarifying agent for a better understanding of world affairs. When Christ was here, in person, before . . . He told them to 'Be ye therefore perfect even as your Father which is in Heaven is perfect' (Matt. 5:48).

"This time, He will teach men the method whereby this possibility can become accomplished fact—through the constant return of the incarnating soul to the school of life on Earth, there to undergo the perfection process of which He was the outstanding example. That is the meaning and teaching of reincarnation."[25]

" 'Whatsoever a man soweth, that shall he also reap' (Gal. 6:7) is a truth which needs reemphasizing. In these words, St. Paul phrases for us the ancient and true teaching of the Law of Cause and Effect, called in the Orient the law of karma.

"The immorality of the human soul, and the innate ability of the spiritual, inner man to work out his own salvation under the Law of Rebirth, in response to the Law of Cause and Effect, are the underlying factors governing all human conduct and all human aspiration. These two laws no man can evade. They condition him at all times until he has achieved the desire and the designed perfection and can manifest on earth as a rightly functioning son of God."[26]

10. The New Age

"The Aquarian Age is preeminently a spiritual age, and the spiritual side of the great lessons that Jesus gave to the world may now be comprehended by multitudes of people, for the many are now coming into an advanced stage of spiritual consciousness. . . ."[27]

---

[25]Bailey, *The Reappearance*, pp. 116–117.
[26]Bailey, *The Reappearance*, p. 147.
[27]Levi, *The Aquarian Gospel*, pp. 10–11.

"As we enter into the New Age, what we are entering into is a cycle, a period of time, a period of unfoldment when truly humanity is the world initiate, the world saviour, and ultimately it is upon the shoulders of humanity that the future and the translation for the entry into light of this planet rest.

"Its meaning as a new age is that for the first time in human history we have a chance to take up a conscious creative recognition of this fact and can begin acting upon it. Up to this time we have moved with evolution. Now comes the time to become the servants of evolution and through our own consciousness to release the light, the love, and the wisdom that will bring our renunciation of spiritual estate (i.e., an attitude of self-sacrifice, to 'give up the good in order to get the best') to its fruition in the occult redemption of the world."[28]

[28]Spangler, *Reflections*, p. 11.

Chapter 3

Biblical Answers to New Age Teachings

There are many different answers that have been given to New Age teachings, for the Church has been on the front lines resisting the occult for almost 2,000 years. It is fair to say that most modern errors are only ancient heresies and doctrines in a different guise, tailor-fitted for the age in which we live.

Therefore it should not surprise us that the old answers from the accumulated wisdom and theological expertise of the apostles, Church Fathers, and reformers are the best means of fighting ancient occultism in its modern forms. It is difficult, if not impossible, to improve on what the historic scholarship of the Christian Church has to say about the revival of occultism in the New Age Cult.

The Personal, Triune God

In New Age theology, the triune God of the Bible cannot be properly described in personal terms. ". . . He is not one

individual, but an energy gestalt."[1] God is seen as an impersonal energy field whose only real personal structure is the
sum of *its* parts. Both Judaism and Christianity abominate
this essentially Hindu concept, affirming an unshakable mon-
otheism—a personal, benevolent, and loving Deity who is immanent within His creation and yet transcends it by infinity
because He is its Creator.

The greatest authorities on the nature and identity of God
are His Son and His Word. Jesus Christ is the living Word of
God and the Bible is the written Word of God. Both testify
that the highest of all truths is the unity of Deity. The great
commandment is this: "Hear, O Israel: the Lord our God,
the Lord is one" (Deut. 6:4; Mark 12:29, NIV).

Christian scholars down through the centuries have recognized the fact that if Jesus Christ does not know God's
nature, and someone else claims that he does, it is readily
apparent that the challenger has placed himself above Christ.
New Age gurus and avatars make this claim. The Christian
must respond by reviewing the superiority of the life and
influence of Jesus Christ upon this world, a world whose very
calendar is dated by His birth.

That the God of the Bible is a personal Being, that He
designates himself as Creator of the universe, and that the
biblical view of creation is scientifically preferable to all ver-
sions cited by New Age leaders is clear evidence. The view of
the world held by pagan sources upon which the New Age
must draw fails all scientific criteria.

The characters and the attributes of the Creator are detailed in the Old and the New Testament, and they bear re-
peating.

In the third chapter of Exodus, Moses encountered God
in the burning bush experience, and God identified himself
as a personal being, saying, "I am the God of thy father, the
God of Abraham, the God of Isaac, and the God of Jacob. . . .I Am that I Am" (Gen. 3:6, 14).

When Moses persisted in asking questions such as "when
I return to the land of Egypt, whom shall I say has sent me?"

---

[1]Jane Roberts, *The Seth Material* (Englewood Cliffs, N.J.: Prentice-Hall, 1970), p. 237.

God responded by saying, "Thus shalt thou say unto the children of Israel, I Am has sent me unto you" (Ex. 3:14).

Jewish scholars have properly translated this as "the Eternal," since God affirmed "this is my name for ever and my memorial to all generations" (Ex. 3:15).

Contrary to what the New Age Cult declares, God is a personal spirit (John 4:24). He has told us, "I am the almighty God; walk before me, and be thou perfect" (Gen. 17:1).

This eternal God revealed himself in the Bible as the Father, the Son, and the Holy Spirit (Matt. 28:19).

The God of creation has reflective memory: "For I know the thoughts that I think toward you, saith the Lord . . ." (Jer. 29:11).

He affirms His uniqueness: "I am the Lord: that is my name: and my glory will I not give to another" (Isa. 42:8).

The knowledge possessed by this all-powerful being is declared to be without limitation: "God . . . knoweth all things" (1 John 3:20).

He possesses a will (Rom. 12:2) to which even His Son is subject: "Lo, I come . . . to do thy will, O God" (Heb. 10:7).

Far from the triune God being "Father-Mother-Child" as the New Age movement maintains, the personal living God proclaims, "I am the first, and I am the last; and beside me there is no God" (Isa. 44:6).

God the Creator loves us; God the Creator remembers us and will tolerate no interference with His decrees. As the Lord Jesus said, "Thy kingdom come. Thy will be done in earth, as it is in heaven" (Matt. 6:10).

The God of the Bible is also the Judge of the universe. Ezekiel writes, "Therefore thus saith the Lord God unto them; Behold, I, even I, will judge . . ." (Ezek. 34:20; Acts 17:31).

The Apostle Paul draws our attention to the fact that we must all appear before the judgment seat of Christ (2 Cor. 5:10), and that all kingdoms will come under the absolute control of His kingdom, and His reign will be everlasting (Rev. 11:15).

These are just some of the descriptions given in Scripture, but they are more than adequate to reveal the sharp contrast that exists between gods fashioned in the image of men or Satan, and "the living God, who is the Savior of all men, especially of those that believe" (1 Tim. 4:10).

Often New Age cultists will say that they reject the biblical concept of God and even the authority of the Scriptures, but their inconsistency surfaces because they persist in quoting scriptures to buttress their own position. Why quote for proof what you say is untrustworthy? The truth is they find it impossible to function without some foundational reference to the eternal God, and we should not hesitate to cite examples of their use of the Bible as proof of inconsistency and lack of spiritual and scholastic integrity.

Jesus Christ

New Age teaching concerning Jesus Christ, though varied, has basic areas of agreement. No New Age cultist will accept Jesus Christ "as the one and only Son of God sacrificed by His loving Father to save humanity from the results of its sins."[2]

The New Age Cult's attack upon the person of Jesus Christ—and attack is surely what it is—concentrates on Christ's unique claim to deity. The Lord Jesus is indeed proclaimed in the New Testament as "the one and only Son of God" by virtue of the Greek term *monogeneses* (cf. John 1:1, 14, 18; 3:16). The second person of the Trinity does not share His throne with Krishna, Buddha, Mohammed, Zoroaster, or any of the endless assortment of gurus and gods. As the Savior of the world, He bore our sins in His own body upon the cross (1 Pet. 2:24), and His miraculous powers have never been duplicated; He is indeed unique among the sons of men.

In answer to those who challenged His identity and authority during His earthly ministry, the Lord Jesus stated, "Even though you do not believe me, believe the miracles" (John 10:38, NIV).

He let the facts speak for themselves. To a questioning John the Baptist in prison, Christ recited the miraculous

---

[2]Benjamin Creme, *The Reappearance of the Christ and the Masters of Wisdom* (London: The Tara Press, 1980), p. 25.

works He had done. To dispel John's doubt, He said, "Go back and report to John what you hear and see: The blind receive sight, the lame walk, those who have leprosy are cured, the deaf hear, the dead are raised, and the good news is preached to the poor" (Matt. 11:4–5, NIV).

Even today, the verified miracles of Jesus of Nazareth proclaim Him as the Word of God made flesh. New Agers will search in vain for any guru in their history who fed 5,000 people with 5 loaves and 2 fishes, who in front of countless witnesses healed the sick, cleansed lepers, raised the dead, opened the eyes of the blind and the ears of the deaf, cast out demons, and demonstrated the love of God for the poor in so many wonderful ways. And how many of them have ever walked on water?

There is good reason for the great antipathy toward the historic Christ and biblical revelation in the New Age. Jesus simply defies all their categories and humbles all their works. This He does precisely because He is the unique Son of God. The New Testament record testifies that He received the worship of men (John 20:28), that He is our great God and Savior (Titus 2:13), that He conquered death itself (Matt. 28:1), and with the coming of His Spirit at Pentecost illumined the world as a flaming torch. That flame has spread to the ends of the earth and burns brightly, even now.

The man from Nazareth was not just an extraordinarily good person, prophet, or sage indwelt by the Christ or Cosmic Consciousness, as the New Age proclaims. He is the King of kings and the Lord of lords, Creator of all ages (Heb. 1:1–3), and He remains the Way, the Truth and the Life. No one comes to the Father but by Him (John 14:6).

The Fallenness of Mankind

It is a cardinal New Age teaching that man is born into this world both good and divine in his nature. Salvation depends upon his looking inward at his spiritual nature and recognizing that he is a god. One New Age writer declares:

> Man as the image of God is already saved with an everlasting salvation. . . . Man is God's image and like-

ness; whatever is possible to God, is possible to man as God's reflection.[3]

The biblical record constantly reflects the fact that man is a sinner, that he has transgressed the law of God. Jesus Christ recognized this and said, "I am not come to call the righteous, but sinners to repentance" (Matt. 9:13).

The Apostle Peter informs us that Christ died for our sins with the purpose of reconciling us, the unjust, to God (1 Pet. 3:18). Paul agrees, writing, "All have sinned and come short of the glory of God. . . . There is none righteous no not one" (Rom. 3:23, 10).

Sin, a transgression of the law, is described as "all unrighteousness" (1 John 5:17), and Isaiah tells us that it was for our transgressions that Jesus the Messiah suffered and died (Isa. 53).

The New Age movement denies the biblical doctrine of sin and substitutes reincarnation as the means of atonement, evading the significance of the cross. But as one New Age writer said, "No one who sees himself as guilty can avoid the fear of God."[4]

It is not that the New Age movement is ignorant of what the Christian Church has been talking about and what Jesus Christ did; it is rather that they refuse to "fear God and keep his commandments" (Eccles. 12:13), and have chosen not to "work the works of God" as God prescribed it should be done (John 6).

The doctrine of personal redemption or salvation from sin is the core of Judaism and Christianity, the oldest monotheistic religions. It is no wonder that such conflict is inevitable, given the New Age movement's definition of salvation. The Apostle John spoke the final word on this when he wrote, "If we confess our sins, he is faithful and just to forgive us our sins, and to cleanse us from all unrighteousness. . . . If we say that we have no sin, we deceive ourselves, and the truth is not in us" (1 John 1:9).

---

[3]Mary Baker Eddy, *Miscellaneous Writings*, pp. 183, 261.
[4]*A Course in Miracles* (Foundation for Inner Peace, 1975), vol. 1, p. 594.

Judgment, Heaven, and Hell

The problem of evil, judgment for wrongdoing, and reward for righteousness are all dealt with in the New Age movement essentially under the concept of reincarnation. According to the law of karma, stated in Christian terms, "whatsoever a man sows, that shall he also reap." New Age teaching eliminates heaven and substitutes Nirvana, the Buddhist idea that all human souls will eventually be absorbed into the great "world soul." Hell is what we reap here in the form of "bad karma" or punishment for errors committed in our past lives. This is as close as the New Age movement gets to the concept of divine judgment.

The Bible describes the judgment when the Lord Jesus Christ will preside and separate the sheep from the goats, the believers from unbelievers. The believers will enter the kingdom of God with heaven as their home, and the others will enter that realm that Jesus said was "prepared for the devil and his angels since the foundation of the ages." Christ also clearly said, "These shall go away into everlasting punishment, but the righteous unto life eternal" (Matt. 25:46).

(For further discussion of this subject, see Chapter 5.)

The Problem of Evil

When discussing the problem of why evil exists and why God allows Satan and demonic powers to have any control in this world, the New Age movement takes a very definite stand:

> It is important to see that Lucifer, as I am using this term, described an angel, a being, a great mighty planetary consciousness. It does not describe the popular thought form of satan who leads man down the path of sin and wrongdoing. . . . Man is his own satan just as man is his own salvation.[5]

In recognizing Lucifer as a "planetary consciousness,"

---

[5]David Spangler, *Reflections on the Christ* (Moray, Scotland: Findhorn Publications, 1978), p. 39.

New Age writers acknowledge the biblical story of the origin of evil and, probably quite unconsciously, adopt biblical descriptions of Satan.

In New Age theology, Satan becomes the "other dark side of the Force," to put it in the vernacular of George Lucas's *Star Wars*. This Force fills the entire universe and sustains it by virtue of the fact that it is one with the universe. Benjamin Creme can thus write quite blithely:

> Of course, yes, the forces of evil are part of God. They are not separate from God. Everything is God.[6]

However, the Bible paints quite a different picture of the Force. The Bible emphatically describes Satan as "the god of this age" (2 Cor. 4:4, NIV), or in the words of Jesus, "the prince of this world" (John 12:31). He is labeled "a murderer from the beginning" (John 8:44) and "the enemy of his Maker" (Isa. 14:13–14). His titles "son of the morning" (Isa. 14:12) and "covering cherub" (Ezek. 28:14) tell us that he fell from a place of great glory and power. After his ejection from heaven, he assumed the title "prince of the power of the air" (Eph. 2:2).

With his great power and alleged benevolence he entered the Garden of Eden and but for divine grace would have destroyed the Creation that God had designed in His own image and likeness.

Because of his evil acts, he will inevitably be defeated by the last Adam, the "Lord from heaven" (1 Cor. 15:47–49), who is the manifest "seed of the woman" (Gen. 3:15). The New Testament proclaims the Lord Jesus Christ to be this seed who will finally defeat Satan and cast him into the lake of fire (Rev. 20:10).

The New Testament fairly bristles with the activities of a personal Satan, not the empty creation of New Age thinking. It was this personal entity who both tempted the Lord Jesus Christ and resisted Him during His years of earthly ministry (Luke 4).

The Lord Jesus has given the Church power over these

---

[6]Creme, *The Reappearance of Christ*, p. 103.

demons in His name (Luke 9:1). Paul urges us to arm ourselves for spiritual warfare against the prince of darkness.
Satan arrays himself as an angel of light so that if it were
possible he would deceive even the chosen of God. The Apostle Paul describes his final deception as "the man of sin . . .
who opposeth and exalteth himself above all that is called
God . . . so that he as God will sit in the temple of God, showing that he is God" (2 Thess. 2). The thirteenth chapter of
the book of Revelation catalogs his persecution of the Church
during the first part of the tribulation that will test the whole
earth, and John shows him broken and defeated eternally
with all his followers (Rev. 20).

The New Age movement fails to recognize that the so-
called "higher beings" masquerading as divine avatars (messengers) or even as the spirits of the dead are in reality fallen
angels directly controlled by Satan and his avowed enemies
of the church of Jesus Christ.

Mahareeshi Mahesh Yoga, in his meditations, speaks of
studying the Hindu scriptures and transcendental meditation
for the purpose of getting in contact with "higher beings or
gods" on other planes of spiritual reality.

The words of the Bible return with awesome force: "The
things which the Gentiles sacrifice, they sacrifice to devils" (1
Cor. 10:20) and "For though there be those that are *called*
gods, whether in heaven or in earth . . . to us there is but one
God, the Father, of whom are all things, and we in him; and
one Lord Jesus Christ" (1 Cor. 8:5–6).

New Agers employ the tools of the occult (tarot cards,
crystals, Ouija boards, mediums or channelers, astrologers,
and fortune tellers) and are in reality seeking after the powers
of "the god of this age." We need to remember the old proverb: "He that would sup with Satan had best have a long
spoon." Practices such as astral projection—leaving your
physical body during sleep to travel to other realms of reality,
as taught by some New Age groups (Eckankar, for example)—place the soul in jeopardy and enter that dimension of
spiritual darkness ruled by Satan, the enemy of all righteousness (cf. Eph. 6:11–12).

The occultic prophet Nostrodamus predicted that in 1999

a great and powerful world leader would arise, subduing all things to himself. It may well be that the Antichrist will be a figure like Maitreya who will succeed in consolidating all authority and then reveal himself with "all powers, signs and lying wonders" (2 Thess. 2:9), deluding the world with his evil charisma.

No matter how all these things may occur, they will come to pass, and behind it all will be those described by the Apostle Paul as "false apostles, deceitful workers, transforming themselves into the apostles of Christ. And no marvel; for Satan himself is transformed into an angel of light. Therefore it is no great thing if *his* ministers also be transformed as the ministers of righteousness; whose end shall be according to their works" (2 Cor. 11:13–15). The New Age Cult fits that description, and only time will reveal the extent of its power.

The Second Coming of Christ

Down through the ages the doctrine of the resurrection of Jesus Christ has plagued the enemies of Christianity. It has been attacked vigorously in every era because it is both the cornerstone and capstone of the Christian faith. This doctrine is inextricably bound up with the doctrine of our Lord's second coming to deliver His church from persecution and to punish with flaming fire and everlasting ruination those who "obey not the gospel of our Lord Jesus Christ" (2 Thess. 1:6–10).

New Age theology attempts to blunt this cosmic event by either spiritualizing it, connecting it with the appearance of "divine messengers" such as Maitreya, or attempting to point to a specific event as its fulfillment. David Spangler, a respected New Age writer, put it another way:

> In a very real sense, Findhorn represents the second coming.[7]

This is perfectly acceptable from the perspective of the New Age world view, which ignores the historic person of

---

[7]Spangler, *Reflections*, p. 10.

Jesus Christ and the fact that He personally promised, "I will come again, and receive you unto myself; that where I am, there ye may be also" (John 14:3).

The picture of Christ descending from the clouds of heaven as John records in Revelation 1, and Paul in 1 Thessalonians 4, is directly dependent upon the doctrine of the resurrection of Christ. Repeatedly in the New Testament, Christ prophesied His bodily resurrection from the dead, not His reincarnation! (Matt. 20:19; Mark 8:3; 9:31; 10:34).

One of the most powerful passages on this subject and the only one that describes the nature of the Resurrection is found in the second chapter of John's gospel. After Christ had cleansed the temple in Jerusalem and the Jews sought a sign from Him to justify His authority in performing that act. He answered them, " 'Destroy this temple, and I will raise it again in three days.' The Jews replied, 'It has taken forty-six years to build this temple, and you are going to raise it in three days?' But the temple he had spoken of was his *body*" (John 2:19–21).

Since we may assume that the disciples and apostles of Christ were men like ourselves—capable of rational, logical thought—we can assume that if Jesus did not come back from the dead in His own body in three days, He would have been considered a false prophet by Old Testament standards and worthy of rejection by His followers. It is significant that John 2:22 reminds us that the apostles remembered this statement about raising the temple when Christ rose from the dead and appeared to them with "infallible proofs" (Acts 1:3).

New Agers tend to think that if the Resurrection took place at all, it was a spirit resurrection portending the future reincarnation of the Christ or Cosmic Consciousness. They are in no way prepared to confess Christ's bodily resurrection.

Since New Age writers talk about the spiritual survival of the Christ after the death of His body, the only records that they can turn to are the accounts of His appearances after that event. Considering Luke 24, we must note that Christ said concerning himself that a spirit does not have flesh and bones as He had—and this came in response to the disciples

perceiving Him as only a spirit. A rational person must reject
the New Age redefinition of the Resurrection on the basis of
what the Scriptures show us.

The gospel of John records that Christ appeared to His
disciples and the apostles, even presenting *His body* for ex-
amination to Thomas the doubter (John 20:24–28), thus con-
firming the prophecy of John 2 with unimpeachable verifi-
cation. In a word, Christ refuted all arguments about the
nature of His resurrection and the fact of His resurrection
by just being there! The Apostle Paul tells us in 1 Corinthians
15 that Christ was raised from the dead and "he appeared to
more than five hundred of the brothers at the same time,
most of whom are still living" (1 Cor. 15:6, NIV). It is no
wonder that Satan and those who are under his captive control (2 Tim.2:26) fear the resurrection of Jesus Christ. It is
the seal of the Church's redemption and of Satan's own judgment.

The Age of Aquarius fears above all else the preaching
of the gospel of Jesus Christ and the fact of His resurrection.
Hindu philosophy and Christian revelation stand face to face
today on the spiritual battleground of time and eternity; but
the battle is the Lord's (1 Sam. 17:47), God's kingdom will
come, and His will be done on earth as it is in heaven.

Let us prepare "to give reason for the hope that lies within
us"; let us study the Scriptures, our constant source of
strength, under the guidance of the Spirit that inspired them
and resist the devil, and he will flee from us. In the words of
a great hymn of the Church:

> Crown Him the Lord of life, who triumphed o'er
> the grave;
> Who rose victorious to the strife for those He came
> to save.
> His glories now we sing who died and rose on high;
> Who died eternal life to bring and lives that death
> may die.

Chapter 4

Dangers of the New Age: A Shadow of Jonestown

Jim Jones, a minister in the Disciples of Christ denomination, led a large number of his church family to death by poison in the jungles of Guyana. This was sparked by his assassination of a sincerely inquisitive congressman and other members of the politician's party during their visit to the headquarters of the cult in Guyana.

Any serious analysis of the dangers of the New Age movement must take into consideration the tragic lesson of Jonestown, where 915 followers of Jones and a concerned senator investigating the cult became the victims of a fanatic influenced by New Age teachings.

This celebrated tragedy of cultic deception and murder in 1978 can be traced unerringly to the New Age doctrines of man's divinity and the relativistic world view of the New Age Cult.

This little known fact has been omitted by all studies of the New Age. It is, however, important and must be analyzed.

Let me hasten to add that Jones was the exception among cultists, *not* the rule. But he was significantly influenced by

the New Age and sadly gave in to those ideas with awful
consequences. Jones carried some of the teachings to terri-
fying, illogical conclusions.

The Missing Link:
Father Divine and the Peace Mission Movement

In the aftermath of Jonestown, we discovered that Jim
Jones had been an admirer and imitator of a Philadelphia-
based cult leader who had proclaimed himself *Father Divine*.

Father Divine, whose real name was George Baker, was
born the son of slaves at a plantation on Hutchinson Island
in Georgia. In 1914, in Valdosta, Georgia, George Baker was
arrested and jailed as a "public menace." Since Baker refused
to give his right name, the court writ stated, *The people* v. *John
Doe, alias God.*

The jury found Baker "not crazy enough to be sent to the
state sanitarium, but crazy enough to be ordered to leave the
State of Georgia." Thus the future god made a hurried exodus from the ungrateful state. From Valdosta, Baker led a
little band of followers to New York City, where he arrived
in 1915 and joined forces with a gentleman known as St. John
the Divine Hickerson, who had a successful work called the
Church of the Living God. Baker learned how to organize
his group from Hickerson and, though terribly lacking in
formal education, became an apt pupil in the art of "godhood."

After much deliberation, Baker bought a two-story frame
house for $2,500 at 72 Macon Street in the all-white com-
munity of Sayville, Long Island, and proceeded to move in.
The deed to this house carried the names of Major J. Divine
and his wife Penniah.

George Baker, following Hickerson, believed quite liter-
ally in 1 Cor. 3:16, which refers to believers as the "temple of
God"; so he reasoned that since God dwelt in him, he was
God and entitled to divine authority. Baker became known
as "the messenger," bearing the exalted title "God and the
Sonship Degree."

To support and expand his work, Father Divine instituted

communal living among his followers, taking the wages of the people of the commune to finance food and shelter for a growing number of people.

After 1929, there were many empty stomachs that would willingly hail as divine anyone who would fill them. He moved from Sayville to Harlem and there, during the Great Depression, fed hundreds of thousands of people and rode the crest of the Harlem popularity wave. After Baker took the name "Father Divine," he accepted worship from his followers. It was common for his devotees to laud him with such words as "Bless your holy heart, Father Dear. Your children are happy knowing you are a god at hand and not a sky-god afar off."

Father Divine's followers claimed that he had died almost 2,000 years ago in the form of Jesus of Nazareth, and that the nineteenth century manifestation of God was not to be the return of Jesus Christ in power, as Scripture so clearly describes it (Rev. 1:7–8), but in the form of a crusader against racial intolerance and false information about the true nature of God.

Father Divine approved. He preached:

> Why believe in something that they say can save you after passing from this existence to keep you living in poverty, debauchery, lacks, wants, and limitations while on this earth you are tabernacling. I will not only lift you as my true believers, but I shall lift humanity from all superstition and cause them to forget all about that imaginary God I am now eradicating and dispelling from the consciousness of the people.

Baker blasphemously affirmed:

> I shall fulfill the Scriptures to the letter and you may tell all the critics and the accusers and blasphemers when they speak maliciously and antagonistically concerning me that I am the Holy Ghost personified! Whether they believe it or not is immaterial to me, for all shall feel the results of the thoughts they think and speak concerning me.[1]

---

[1] *The New Day*, July 16, 1949.

This is the mission for which I came. It is written, "The government shall be upon His shoulders, He shall be called Wonderful Counselor, the Mighty God, the Everlasting Father."

Why do you call me Father? God Almighty! Thunders a response from thousands. Now isn't that wonderful! And Prince of Peace! Why do you say peace around here? Because the Prince of Peace has been recognized.[2]

In a personal letter directed to Mr. Kenneth Daire, written on March 16, 1949, Father Divine stated:

Thus the greater the opposition, the more I advance, and the more my deity is observed the more I prove my omnipotence, omniscience, and omnipresence. And I prove my mastery over all flesh, for if I were not God I would have long since failed.

His publications reveal that he found foundational basis for his teachings in the writings by the Unity School of Christianity. In some instances, the language of the Unity and Father Divine publications is identical. The Unity School (founded in 1891) was heavily influenced by Hinduism and Theosophy, teaching the New Age concept that man is essentially deity and needs only to recognize that fact in order to be freed from the limitations of this existence. Father Divine believed and taught the same thing, combining this with a genuine effort to feed, clothe, and shelter people during the Great Depression of the 1930s.

Social work was the great emphasis of Father Divine, but he also crusaded against racial prejudice, which he combined with the teaching that he was God. Concerning racial prejudice he stated:

If the prejudiced and antagonistic employers refuse to have you in their service just because of your belief in me and your conviction of my deity, they will suffer even as Sodom and Gomorrah did, in whom righ-

---

[2]*The Spoken Word*, June 16, 1936.

teousness was not found sufficient to save them. . . .

So it is the same spirit, the same one you have been praying to that I am in the body now, and I am summed up and recognized in this body to reach them and to save them of every undesirable condition. That is such a glorious privilege! Even as you see it in my office now you would, or could not, have thought that such an expression as being termed different races and colors could be united together in the unity of the spirit of mind, of aim, and of purpose until I came personally! But I came to let you and all mankind know that "out of one blood God created all nations of men for to dwell upon the face of the whole earth."[3]

Jim Jones was attracted by the communal lifestyle of Father Divine's Peace Mission movement and took bus loads of his people there to observe how it functioned. He was impressed with Father Divine's capacity to provide funds by means of communal living and to carry out what he considered to be the Christian imperative of the Good Samaritan, taking care of one's neighbor. Surely no one can fault either Father Divine or Jim Jones for pursuing the Christian ethic and doctrine of "loving our neighbor as ourselves" (Lev. 19:18). But as history has shown, it did not end there.

George Baker affirmed his divinity in terms of the New Age, and through his publications, he urged his followers to recognize themselves as his children. These are the things that Jim Jones absorbed and put into practice in San Francisco.

Eyewitness accounts tell of how Jones would begin by quoting from the Bible in his hand. Later, as he shifted emphasis from the Bible to himself as the messenger of God, he would throw the Bible on the ground and kick it because he considered his authority as the representative of deity to be superior to the written Word of God. One psychologist I interviewed who had worked at the headquarters of the People's Temple in San Francisco said that Jones would use pseudo-Pentecostal fervor, expressions, and illustrations to

---

[3]*The New Day*, July 1949.

inflame his audience until, as she put it, "he became God's substitute to them."

George Baker had followed exactly the same procedures with the equally corrupt theology. The link was forged.

The mass suicide at Jonestown began with the recognition of an authority higher than God and His Word, an authority self-conferred by a spiritual child of Father Divine's Peace Mission movement. The work that George Baker and Jim Jones had done in fighting racial prejudice was admirable, but without the steadying force of God's Spirit and His Word, it too became perverted to the point that the initial beneficiaries become the victims in the end.

Father Divine, like Jim Jones, was taken with Marxist philosophy. They espoused the idea of the motto "From each according to his ability, to each according to his need." Baker flirted with the Communist movement for over eight years and once stated in glowing terms:

> I stand for anything that will deal justly between men and man. The Communists stand for social equality and for justice in every issue and this is a principle for which I stand. I am not representing religion. I am representing God on earth and among men and I will cooperate with an organization that will stand for the right and will deal justly.

In *The New Day*, Divine's propaganda newspaper, he spoke of his cooperation with the Communists, while at the same time affirming his uniqueness: "Every knee shall bow and every tongue confess that Father Divine is God, God, God."

By 1941, Father Divine's admiration for the Communists had worn rather thin. Their relationship came to an abrupt end in that year, and Father Divine described the Communists as unamerican and ungodly. By the time the Korean war broke out in 1950, he freely declared himself "a righteous fighter against the forces of communism."

We now know that Jim Jones was intrigued with Marxism and even attempted to bribe the Russian ambassador to Guyana in a vain attempt to leave South America and place himself under Communist rule elsewhere. It appears that Father Divine, becoming aware of what the Communists were all about, had the good sense to jettison his support for them. Jim Jones, even when rebuffed by the Soviets, pursued his courtship with Marxism.

Chapter 5

Dangers of the New Age Today

The manner in which the New Age cult penetrates the various sectors of education, politics, and religion must be reviewed lest we forget the lesson of Jonestown or the New Age's massive influence being exercised on various social fronts.

There are genuine dangers in the New Age movement at all levels of society. Very few people are aware that Robert Kennedy's assassin, Sirhan, was deeply involved with New Age thinking through the writings of the Theosophical Society. The first book he requested when he was imprisoned after killing Robert Kennedy was *The Secret Doctrine*, by Helena Blavatsky, founder of Theosophy.

Madame Blavatsky taught that man was intrinsically divine and had the right to perceive truth from his own vantage point, independent of all others and all evidence to the contrary! Sirhan had been very deeply influenced by this philosophical concept. Since Hinduism views the material world as *Maya*, illusory, a lower form of mind or spirit, and since the law of karma prevails, removing Robert Kennedy was perfectly logical. Bad karma, transgressions from his past lives, would kill him one way or another. Robert Kennedy was dead, just as dead as those at Jonestown.

An undisclosed number of the followers of the New Age Cult do not hesitate to speak of a coming apocalypse that will "cleanse" the earth of those who are in need of "purgation." These blots on the biosphere are typically described as those "less evolved" souls who do not see "all is one" or "all is God."[1]

> There is a material difference . . . between expecting some kind of apocalypse—from which only those who have achieved higher consciousness will emerge unscathed—and claiming to commit the apocalypse yourself. The former is a major theme of New Age thinking, the latter only appears in carefully selected extracts.[2]

In the same article, Boren notes:

> When you combine that expectation of world destruction with reliance on direct revelation from spirit guides and add a philosophy that embraces "do your own thing" as a guiding principle, you are asking for trouble.

Texe Marrs's *Dark Secrets of the New Age* provides over 30 pages of material dealing with this kind of "cleansing." The New Age attitude in this area bodes no good will for historic Christianity.[3]

We would do well to observe events of this nature and analyze, within their context, precisely what the motives of at least certain segments of the New Age Cult are as they vigorously work at penetrating all areas of world culture.

---

[1]Douglas Groothuis, *Confronting the New Age* (Downers Grove, Ill.: InterVarsity Press, 1988), p. 204.

[2]Rebecca Boren, *The Seattle Weekly* (Jan. 7–13, 1987), p. 22.

[3]Texe Marrs, *Dark Secrets of the New Age* (Westchester, Ill.: Crossway Books, 1987), pp. 136–165.

Dangers of the New Age Movement in Education

The Strategic Importance of Education

Abraham Lincoln said, "The philosophy of education in one generation will be the philosophy of government in the next."[4]

Regarding the strategic importance of education, Brooks Alexander, co-founder of the Spiritual Counterfeits Project, says:

> In the ideological contest for cultural supremacy, public education is the prime target; it influences the most people in the most pervasive way at the most impressionable age. No other social institution has anything close to the same potential for mass indoctrination.[5]

> Marilyn Ferguson reported that of the many "Aquarian Conspirators" she surveyed, "more were involved in education than in any other single category of work. They were teachers, administrators, policy makers, and educational psychologists."[6]

The New Age and Textbooks

1. According to Mel and Norma Gabler in their book *What Are They Teaching Our Children?*:

> It is foolish to underestimate the power of textbooks on what students study. Seventy-five percent of students' classroom time and ninety percent of homework time is spent with textbook materials.[7]

2. Paul Vitz conducted a federally funded, systematic

---

[4]Douglas Groothuis, *Confronting the New Age* (Downers Grove, Ill.: InterVarsity Press, 1988), p. 129.
[5]Brooks Alexander, "The Rise of Cosmic Humanism: What Is Religion?" *SCP Journal* (vol. 5, Winter 1981–82), p. 4.
[6]Marilyn Ferguson, *The Aquarian Conspiracy* (Los Angeles: J.P. Tarcher, 1980), p. 280.
[7]Mel and Norma Gabler, *What Are They Teaching Our Children?* (Wheaton, Ill.: Victor Books, 1985), p. 22.

study of the content of public-school textbooks through the
National Institute of Education in 1985. His final conclusion
is disturbing:

> Religion, traditional family values, and conservative
> political and economic positions have been reliably ex-
> cluded from the children's textbooks.[8]

3. Omitting such values from textbooks teaches children
that these values are unimportant. Sir Walter Moberly said:

> It is a fallacy to suppose that by omitting a subject
> you teach nothing about it. On the contrary, you teach
> that it is to be omitted, and that it is therefore a matter
> of secondary importance. And you teach this not
> openly and explicitly, which would invite criticism; you
> simply take it for granted and there-by insinuate it
> silently, insidiously, and all but irresistibly.[9]

The New Age in the Classroom

1. New Age educator Beverly Galyean's *Confluent Education* is dangerous because it leads children to believe that they
are perfect and divine. Since the sin problem is nonexistent
in Galyean's philosophical system, there is obviously no need
for Jesus Christ and what He accomplished at the cross. Her
system builds a false confidence in children because they are
taught that they are godlike. Douglas Groothuis describes one
of Galyean's teaching methods:

> In a Los Angeles public school classroom, 25 first-
> graders lie still as their teacher tells them to imagine
> they are perfect beings who are full of light and who
> contain all of the wisdom of the universe within them.
> This exercise in "guided imagery" is part of educator
> Beverly Galyean's curriculum of "confluent educa-
> tion," and it reflects her belief that "we are all God."[10]

---

[8]Paul Vitz, *Censorship: Evidence of Bias in Our Children's Textbooks* (Ann Arbor, Mich.: Servant, 1986), p. 1.
[9]Richard John Neuhaus, "Belief Is in the Eye of the Beholder," *Religion and Society Report* (August 1986), p. 2.
[10]Douglas Groothuis, *Moody Monthly* (vol. 85, February 1985), p. 20.

The ancients of all cultures filled their folkloric epics with tales of visions, dreams, intuitive insights, and internal dialogues with higher beings whom they say are the sources of ultimate wisdom and knowledge. By accepting as true the narratives of spiritual seekers from all cultures, we now have evidence of various levels of consciousness possible to human beings. From Delphi's "Know thyself," through Scripture's "You shall be as gods!" we are left with the certitude that we are, indeed, multi-dimensional beings capable of works beyond our imagining and that our primary purpose in life is to discover who we are and who we can become.[11]

Once we begin to see that we are all God, that we all have the attributes of God, then I think the whole purpose of human life is to reown the Godlikeness within us; the perfect love, the perfect wisdom, the perfect understanding, the perfect intelligence; and when we do that, we create back to that old, that essential oneness which is consciousness.[12]

2. *Guided imagery* in the classroom is dangerous because it teaches children a way of dealing with problems that leaves God out of the picture.

Susan Pinkston, a pastor's wife in Winter, California, wrote about her ten-year-old son's teacher who had led him and other students through a session of guided imagery:

He said she had them lie on the floor, close their eyes, breathe deeply, and count backward from ten. She then described a journey in which they were walking through a lovely meadow. They walked up the hillside and sprouted wings out their backs. They flew away to a cave; they walked into the cave and saw three doors. They opened one door and the room was filled with their "heart's desire." That room was to go to

---

[11]Beverly Galyean, *Journal of Humanistic Psychology* (vol. 21, no. 4, Fall 1981).
[12]Francis Adeney, "Educators Look East," *Spiritual Counterfeits Journal* (vol. 5, no. 1, Winter 1981), p. 28.

anytime [they were] under stress.[13]

Guided imagery can also open us up to counterfeit christs, or "angels of light" (cf. 2 Cor. 11:14).

Douglas Groothuis comments on guided imagery in his book *Confronting the New Age*:

> An elaborate visualization exercise could induce an altered state of consciousness quite amenable to demonic insurgents. Shakti Gawain, for instance, says that "creative visualization" can easily introduce one to "spirit guides," the likes of which would be thrilled to meet us.[14]

We must also remember that man's imagination is affected by the Fall. Gen. 6:5 says: "And God saw that the wickedness of man was great in the earth, and that every imagination of the thoughts of his heart was only evil continually." If we do not start from this point, we will likely believe anything we find in our subconscious. Visualization can be dangerous, especially as taught by New Agers who deny that man has a sin problem.

3. *Values clarification* in the classroom is dangerous because it denies the existence of moral absolutes from God's Word. Each student is encouraged to come up with his or her own moral values.

Values clarification was pioneered by Louis E. Raths and Sidney B. Simon. The goal of values clarification "is to involve students in practical experiences, making them aware of their own feelings, their own ideas, their own beliefs, so that the choices and decisions they make are conscious and deliberate, based on their own value systems."[15]

The fundamental assumption in values clarification is that there are no absolute truths. Values are considered to be essentially neutral. They are to be subjectively chosen by each student. In response to this idea, Richard A. Baer writes:

---

[13]Caryl Matrisciana, *Gods of the New Age* (Eugene, Ore.: Harvest House, 1985), pp. 172–173.

[14]Douglas Groothuis, *Confronting*, p. 183.

[15]Sidney B. Simon, Leland W. Howe, and Howard Kirschenbaum, *Values Clarification* (New York: Hart, 1978), back cover (see also pp. 18–22).

On the deeper level ... the claim to neutrality is entirely misleading. At this more basic level, the originators of values clarification simply assume that their own subjective theory of values is correct. ... If parents object to their children using pot or engaging in premarital sex, the theory behind values clarification makes it appropriate for the child to respond, "But that's just *your* value judgment. Don't force it on me."[16]

4. *Meditation* in the classroom is dangerous. In Eastern meditation, one is taught to empty the mind with the goal of attaining "cosmic consciousness," oneness with all things. This is unlike biblical meditation, which always has an objective focus (such as filling the mind with God's Word).

One book that made its way into a California school district is entitled *Meditating With Children: The Art of Concentration and Centering*, by Deborah Rozman. Its subtitle, "A Workbook on New Age Educational Methods using Meditation," tells us all we need to know about the book.

5. *Globalism* taught in the classroom is dangerous because it is based on a monistic world view that espouses not only the unity of all mankind but a unity of all religious beliefs too.

Two global educators report:

Most educators agree that children should be introduced to global perspectives as early as possible, certainly before the onset of puberty when ethnocentrism and stereotypical thinking tend to increase dramatically.[17]

6. *Yoga* in the classroom is dangerous because all forms of yoga involve occult assumptions, even *hatha yoga*, which is often presented as a strictly physical discipline. Author Douglas Groothuis writes:

Even advocates of yoga report the dangers of the

[16]Richard A. Baer, Jr., "Parents, Schools and Values Clarification," *The Wall Street Journal* (April 12, 1982).
[17]Jacquelyn Johnson and John Benegar, "Global Issues in the Intermediate School," *Social Education* (February 1983), p. 131.

energy (*kundalini*) it may awaken. This may involve insanity, physical burning, sexual aberrations, and so on. Although Paul says that physical discipline is of some use, we should steer clear of yoga.[18]

Robert Griffs testified:

In the fall semester of the school year 1980–81, in Hocker Grove Junior High in Shawnee Mission public schools, there was a P.E. class that . . . used a mandatory or compulsory course in yoga [including vocal repetition of unidentified words, most likely Hindu mantras] to teach the kids to meditate.[19]

In summary, with *confluent education, guided imagery, values clarification, meditation, globalism,* and *yoga* making their way into schools, it becomes clear that the New Age movement has made significant inroads into the educational system. This has profound implications for Christian parents with children in public schools. Parents must become informed about their child's activities in school, and take action when necessary.

The New Age in Curriculum

1. A description of the nature and purpose of New Age education is provided by Jack Canfield and Paula Klimek:

The word "education" comes from the Latin word *educare* (to lead out from within). What teachers are now interested in leading out from within is the expression of the self—the highest qualities of the individual student's unique soul.[20]

2. Marilyn Ferguson shares her thoughts on the new curriculum:

---

[18]Douglas Groothuis, *Unmasking the New Age* (Downers Grove, Ill.: InterVarsity Press, 1986), p. 68.
[19]Phyllis Schlafly, ed., *Child Abuse in the Classroom* (Westchester, Ill.: Crossway Books, 1984), pp. 209–210.
[20]Jack Canfield and Paula Klimek, "Education in the New Age," *New Age* (February 1978), p. 270.

Altered states of consciousness are taken seriously: "centering" exercises, meditation, relaxation, and fantasy are used to keep the intuitive pathways open and the whole brain learning. Students are encouraged to "tune in," imagine, and identify the special feeling of peak experiences. There are techniques to encourage body awareness: breathing, relaxation, yoga, movement, and biofeedback.[21]

3. Ferguson also says that curriculum is geared toward autonomy. But this covers not only the positive shouldering of personal responsibility but even rebellious independence:

A major ambition of the curriculum is autonomy. This is based on the belief that if our children are to be free, they must be free even from us, from our limiting beliefs and our acquired tastes and habits. At times this means teaching for healthy, appropriate rebellion, not conformity.[22]

Ferguson quotes an old Hebrew proverb as the basis for setting children free to find their own path: "Do not confine your children to your own learning, for they were born in another time."[23]

4. The innocence of New Age terminology makes the cult's basic ideas readily acceptable. According to New Age activist Dick Sutphen:

One of the biggest advantages we have as New Agers is, once the occult, metaphysical and New Age terminology is removed, we have concepts and techniques that are very acceptable to the general public. So we can change the names to demonstrate the power. In so doing, we open the door to millions who normally would not be receptive.[24]

Jack Canfield and Paul Klimek advise their fellow edu-

---

[21] Ferguson, *The Aquarian Conspiracy*, p. 315.
[22] Ibid., p. 316.
[23] Ibid., p. 320.
[24] Dick Sutphen, "Infiltrating the New Age Into Society," *What Is* (Summer 1986), p. 14.

cators on how to present meditation:

> Centering can also be extended into work with med-
> itation in the classroom. (Advice: if you're teaching in
> a public school, don't call it meditation, call it "center-
> ing." Every school wants children to be relaxed, atten-
> tive, and creative, and that is what they will get).[25]

Dangers of the New Age Movement in Politics

The New Age Political Agenda

1. The New Age political agenda is dangerous because it
regards the present political structure/goals/methods as obsolete and ineffective in achieving the needs of humanity.

> The political system needs to be transformed, not
> reformed. We need something else, not just something
> more.[26]

2. New Agers are working toward a centralizing of power
on a global level. Physicist Fritjof Capra writes:

> During the second half of our century it has become
> increasingly apparent that the nation-state is no longer
> workable as an effective unit of governance. It is too
> big for the problems of its local populations and, at
> the same time, confined by concepts too narrow for
> the problems of global interdependence. Today's
> highly centralized national governments are able nei-
> ther to act locally nor to think globally. Thus political
> decentralization and regional development have been
> urgent needs of all large countries. This decentrali-
> zation of economic and political power will have to
> include a redistribution of production and wealth, to
> balance foods and populations within countries and
> between the industrial nations and the Third World.[27]

---

[25]Jack Canfield and Paula Klimek, "Education."
[26]Ferguson, *The Aquarian Conspiracy*, p. 191.
[27]Fritjof Capra, *The Turning Point* (New York: Simon and Schuster, 1982), p. 398.

New Age political methodology should be of concern to all of us because it is both *outwardly aggressive* and *quietly subtle* in its penetration of society.

New Age Groups

Some examples of outwardly aggressive New Age groups penetrating society are:

The Green Party—The Green Party is a growing political power that seeks to challenge traditional politics by emphasizing issues such as ecology, feminism, and disarmament. "Green parties are active in every nation in Western Europe, many Asian countries, Canada, Mexico, Costa Rica, Argentina, and Brazil. In the United States, approximately one hundred local Green groups are linked through a national network and clearing-house, the Committees of Correspondence."[28]

Greenpeace U.S.A.—Greenpeace is a nonprofit environmental organization with over 2.5 million supporters worldwide. The ultimate goal of the group is to engender a "planetary consciousness" in the world. They promote ocean ecology, disarmament, and the prevention of toxic pollution. They accomplish their goals by two means: educating people and legislative lobbying. Greenpeace is thoroughly New Age and affirms that "our ultimate goal . . . is to help bring about that basic change in thinking known as 'planetary consciousness.' "[29]

Planetary Citizens—This is an activist group committed to engendering "planetary consciousness" among New Age groups, the general public, and world leaders. Donald Keys says of Planetary Citizens:

> Our goal is largely to try to orchestrate . . . a general awakening, a crossing of the threshold to global awareness . . . for as large a part of the population of the world as we can. . . . There has to be some critical mass

---

[28]*The 1989 Guide to New Age Living* (Winter 1989), p. 111.
[29]Mark Satin, *New Age Politics* (New York: Dell, 1979), p. 331.

of public awareness, of planetary consciousness, before politicians will move, before foreign offices will
get into gear, before teaching changes in the schools.[30]

The Unity-in-Diversity Counsel—This group is a New Age "metanetwork" of over 100 networks and groups. The counsel
promotes global cooperation and interdependence on a
worldwide scale. Elliot Miller comments:

> Unlike traditional Eastern mysticism, which tends to
> be reclusive, the New Age movement is increasingly
> marked by efforts to penetrate society. The force be-
> hind this is an evolving ethic that stresses a balance
> between internal (personal) and external (social)
> "transformation."[31]

New Age Methods of Social Penetration

The methods that the New Age uses to penetrate every
level of our social structure are subtle. They differ drastically
from the actions of the aggressive groups in that they tend
to be very socially acceptable.

Infiltration—There are many groups like the Sierra Club, Am-
nesty International, and Zero Population Growth, which are
not New Age. Nevertheless, New Agers may be in their ranks
working to win over their co-workers to their planetary perspective. Donald Keys writes:

> We can help to "planetize" existing organizations
> and groups by joining with them in their efforts to
> promote human rights, peace, and "soft energy
> paths"; while working with them we can contribute the
> world-inclusive perspective.[32]

Networks—"So why don't we hear more about New Age activ-
ism? One answer is that much of that movement's strength
lies in its informal, low profile networks."[33]

---

[30]Donald Keys, "All About Planetary Citizens: A Seminar in Four Parts."
[31]Elliot Miller, "Saying No to the New Age," *Moody Monthly* (February 1985), p. 22.
[32]Donald Keys, *Earth at Omega* (Boston: Branden Press, 1982), p. 101.
[33]Elliot Miller, "Saying No to the New Age" *Moody Monthly* (February 1985), p. 24.

Related to the above, New Age political methodology is of great concern because of its effective use of networks of people and groups. Such networks, largely unrecognized by the general populace, are growing in power and influence. Because of this, Christians may be blind to the political power of the New Age movement. But the danger is real. As one New Age writer tells us:

The Aquarian Conspiracy is . . . a network of many networks aimed at social transformation.[34]

These networks are often unpretentious organizations. Jessica Lipnack and Jeffrey Stamps tell us that networks are "spontaneously created by people to address problems and offer possibilities primarily outside of established institutions."[35]

But networks wield significant political power. Marilyn Ferguson writes:

It generates power enough to remake society. It offers the individual emotional, intellectual, spiritual, and economic support. It is an invisible home, a powerful means of altering the course of institutions, especially government.

Anyone who discovers the rapid proliferation of networks and understands their strength can see the impetus for worldwide transformation.[36]

Though New Age groups are autonomous, their combined efforts make all the difference in accomplishing a common goal. Lipnack and Stamps write:

The many perspectives of a network derive from the autonomy of its members. All have their own turf and agendas, yet they cooperate in the network because they also have some common values and visions.[37]

---

[34]Ferguson, *The Aquarian Conspiracy*, p. 217.
[35]Jessica Lipnack and Jeffrey Stamps, *Networking* (Garden City, N.Y.: Doubleday & Company, 1982), p. 7.
[36]Ferguson, *The Aquarian Conspiracy*, p. 213.
[37]Lipnack Stamps, *Networking*, p. 227.

Donald Keys, who is involved in the New Age drive for world peace, says:

> One of the most important things that is happening is . . . networking. . . . A lot of us are on Peacenet (an international computer-based communications and information sharing system for "peace" activists) with our PC computers. There is a gathering awareness that we won't all have to be doing the same thing but we need to be knowing what each other is doing. . . . I believe that awareness is finally hitting reality now, and is taking form.[38]

Summary

As we have noted, the New Age movement has many faces; and specific dangers accompany each of these faces within the fields of education, politics, and religion. Elliot Miller's words effectively warn us about the purpose of the New Age movement:

> New Agers may differ over such questions as when the New Age begins, whether it will be preceded by a worldwide cataclysm, how it will be politically struc- tured, whether there will be a Christ-figure governing it, or who the true avatars [god-men] or messengers from the spirit world are. Nonetheless, they agree that they can hasten the new order that they all await by cooperating to influence developments in our cul- ture's political, economic, social, and spiritual life.[39]

---

[38]Donald Keys and Willis Harman, *Sharing Personal and Planetary Security*, tape (San Anselmo, Calif.: Conference Coordinating Company, 1986).
[39]Elliot Miller, "The New Age Movement: What Is It?" *Forward* (Summer 1985), p. 18.

Chapter 6

The
New Age
Agenda

There is a danger that New Age thought may cause some Christians to develop a paranoia about anything appearing to be associated with the movement, especially in regard to conspiracy theories. But as the old joke says, "Just because you're paranoid doesn't mean they're *not* really after you!"

The New Age political agenda is dangerous because it is based on a *monistic and pantheistic* world view. As such, the New Age political agenda is anti-theistic and anti-Christian. Mark Satin, author of *New Age Politics*, says:

Planetary consciousness recognizes our oneness with all humanity and in fact with all life, everywhere, and with the planet as a whole.[1]

The destiny of mankind, after its long preparatory period of separation and differentiation, is at last to become one.... This unity is on the point of being politically expressed in a world government that will

---

[1]Mark Satin, *New Age Politics* (New York: Dell, 1979), p. 148.

unite nations and regions in transactions beyond their individual capacity.[2]

New Age prophet David Spangler writes:

Certainly the politics of synergy will reinterpret humanity's relationship to nature, to the use of natural resources, its relationships with animals and plants, and to everything that makes up the environment. . . . In a group and in a group of groups where the awareness of separation is dispelled and an awareness of oneness, of unity and of dynamic cooperation and goodwill is substituted, the whole spectrum of international and national politics as we know it must disappear and be transformed into something quite unrecognizable by today's standards.[3]

Monism and pantheism are the metaphysical base on which the New Age movement rests. Every major cultural transformation rests on a shift in world views. Lewis Mumford observes the importance of this new ideology. He says that "every transformation of man, except perhaps that which produced the neolithic culture, has rested on a new metaphysical and ideological base—or rather, upon deeper stirrings and intuitions whose rationalized expression takes the form of a new picture of the cosmos and the nature of man."[4]

Unity of Religions

The new ideological base of the New Age political agenda is a *unity of all religions*. While allowing various religions to exist, each religion is viewed as teaching the same core truth: mankind is divine. Christianity is reinterpreted in this light (New Agers call it "Esoteric Christianity".) A unity of religions is absolutely necessary if the "oneness of mankind" is to become a reality.

---

[2]Ibid., p. 142.
[3]David Spangler, *Explorations: Emerging Aspects of the New Culture* (Forres, Scotland: Findhorn Publications, 1981), p. 85.
[4]Lewis Mumford, *The Transformations of Man* (New York: Harper and Row, 1972), p. 179.

Robert Muller, recently retired U.N. Assistant Secretary General, commented on the unity of religions:

> For the first time in history we have discovered that this is one planet on which we live. Now it remains for us to discover that we are also one human family and that we have to transcend all national, linguistic, cultural, racial, and religious differences which have made our history. We have a chance to write a completely new history.[5]

Related to this is Matthew Fox's concept of *deep ecumenism*. He writes:

> Deep ecumenism is the movement that will unleash the wisdom of all world religions: Hinduism and Buddhism, Islam and Judaism, Taoism and Shintoism, Christianity in all its forms, and native religions and goddess religions throughout the world. This unleashing of wisdom holds the last hope for the survival of the planet we call home.[6]

This wisdom from all religions is seen as centered around a core truth: the divinity of man. Regarding this core truth, David Spangler writes:

> What is seeking to emerge is a body of people who are nourishers and who are quite literally what Jesus called "the salt of the earth," but consciously so, spiritually so, accepting their divinity without becoming inflated by it, and acting within the sphere of their influence to draw that same divinity out of others. . . . These are givers of life, and they are forming the basis for the government of the future.[7]

Unity of Government

The New Age political agenda is also dangerous because it is grounded in a false confidence in *human potential* and not

---

[5]*The Movement Newspaper,* "U.N.'s Robert Muller to Speak at Universal Peace Conference" (February 1983), p. 21.

[6]Matthew Fox, *The Coming of the Cosmic Christ* (New York: Harper & Row, 1988), p. 288.

[7]Spangler, *Explorations,* p. 72.

in dependence on divine guidance. The all-pervading Cosmic Christ fills each man with potential.

Many New Agers believe that the Cosmic Christ has worked in ages past in the lives of great individuals to effect change in the world. The Cosmic Christ can likewise work through all human beings today. Matthew Fox writes:

> Does the fact that the Christ became incarnate in Jesus exclude the Christ's becoming incarnate in others—Lau-tzu or Buddha or Moses or Sarah or Sojourner Truth or Gandhi or me or you? Just the opposite is the case. In fact, Paul's letter to the Galatians talks of the Christ becoming incarnate in him: "I no longer live, but Christ lives in me" (Gal. 2:20, NIV). Paul challenges the recipients of his letter to "form Christ in you" (4:20) and be "sons and daughters of God" (3:27).[8]

The New Age political agenda is dangerous because it does not recognize *moral absolutes* based on God's Word. All moral values are subjectively determined. All is relative. The relativity of all moral values is taught in schools through programs of "values clarification."

The New Age political agenda regarding a *one-world government* is dangerous because it is grounded in man's desire to attain unity with man acting as the sole authority. The political agenda does not recognize the authority of a sovereign and omnipotent God. Douglas Groothuis observes:

> In the New Agers' agenda, they must lay the brick of a new Babel, proclaiming an order whose ultimate unity and direction opposes the Creator (see Gen. 11:1–9). The ancient world-order enthusiasts in Genesis tried to force the "apostate thesis of ultimate oneness and equality onto all mankind" in order to build a "one-world order and usher in paradise apart from God" (Rushdoony 1979). That is what the New Agers are trying to do today, and their attempt is equally in vain. All towers of Babel are built in vain, apart from

---

[8]Fox, *The Coming of the Cosmic Christ*, p. 235.

the cornerstone of Jesus Christ.[9]

The globalized government that is a part of the New Age political agenda espouses a *planetary police force* for security. Only those who subscribe to a monistic and pantheistic world view would be allowed to control this police force.

Planetary Citizens is now sponsoring an "Independent Commission on World Security Alternatives," which is enlisting various peace, disarmament, and systems experts to design a "workable, believable, and nonthreatening global security system."[10]

The source of this unity is relatively clear. Many involved in New Age politics are clearly basing their decisions and actions on *occultic revelations*. For example, many adhere to the writing of Alice Bailey. She often speaks of "The Plan" and the "Masters of the Hierarchy." Ascended Masters are those who have supposedly reached the highest level of consciousness and have become guides of the spiritual evolution of mankind. These Masters are supposedly busy in the outworking of "The Plan" on earth.

World Goodwill is a political lobbying group whose goal is to unfold "The Plan" as spelled out in the many books of Alice Bailey. This is one of several Bailey-oriented groups sponsored by the Lucis Trust.

The globalism that is a part of the New Age political agenda amounts to a form of idolatry. It exalts the planet as well as mankind as sovereign lords. Groothuis comments:

An idolatrous internationalism must be rejected by Christians. Christ is Lord; neither the nations nor the planet are sovereign. Global government, or what could be termed "the cosmic state," must be rejected as idolatry, since cosmic humanism enthrones man in the place of God.[11]

---

[9]Douglas Groothuis, "Politics: Building an International Platform," *The New Age Rage*, ed. by Karen Hoyt and J. Isamu Yamamoto (Old Tappan, N.J.: Revell, 1987), p. 104.
[10]Donald Keys, "Security Alternatives," (*AHP Perspective*, December 1985), p. 18.
[11]Douglas Groothuis, *The New Age Rage*, p. 105.

Dangers of the New Age Movement for the Church

Redefining the Problem: Sin

The New Age political agenda is dangerous because it completely ignores man's greatest problem—*sin*—as well as God's provision for this problem—the substitutionary atonement of Jesus Christ. Douglas Groothuis writes:

> The Christian believes that political realism must begin with the realization that man is a sinner; New Agers hope in human potential, which is viewed as good and trustworthy. The New Age equates sin with ignorance, believing we can rid ourselves of such ignorance when we accept the enlightenment of pantheism.
>
> The Christian sees such enlightenment as a deceptive counterfeit. The only way that either personal or political consciousness can be raised is by first seeing the reality of sin and the need of redemption through Jesus Christ. All detours around the cross of Christ crash on the brutal rocks of reality. The Christian who hungers and thirsts for political justice looks to God as Lord, Lawgiver, and Judge, not to a godhead within. Christians serve the Savior, not the self. They consult the Scriptures for political instruction.[12]

Sin is redefined in New Age thought. Evil is relative. David Spangler writes:

> Man holds the ultimate responsibility for the redemption of what we have come to call "evil energies," which are simply energies that have been used out of timing or out of place, or not suited to the needs of evolution.[13]
>
> [New Age ethics] is not based on . . . dualistic concepts of "good" or "bad."[14]

---

[12]Ibid., p. 101.
[13]David Spangler, *Revelation: The Birth of a New Age* (Middleton: The Lorian Press, 1976), p. 38.
[14]Ibid., p. 13.

New Ager Mark Satin tells us that "in a spiritual state, morality is impossible."[15]

Christ's Work on the Cross

Benjamin Creme rejects orthodox Christianity because it presents "a picture of the Christ impossible for the majority of thinking people today to accept as the One and Only son of God, sacrificed by His Loving Father to save Humanity from the results of its sins; as a Blood Sacrifice straight out of the old and outworn Jewish Dispensation."[16]

Salvation

New Age salvation is a progressive operation. People must work off their bad karma from lifetime to reincarnated lifetime. Shirley MacLaine writes:

If you are good and faithful in your struggle in this life, the next one will be easier.[17]

David Spangler writes that "man is his own Satan just as man is his own salvation."[18]

Subtle Deviations

Creator and Creation

There is a danger of New Age thought blurring the distinction between the Creator and the creation—especially human beings as creatures—in the minds of biblically illiterate believers. This danger is rooted in the monistic nature of New Age thought, which treats all as part of the great god-soul.

Mark Satin, author of *New Age Politics*, says:

Planetary consciousness recognizes our oneness

---

[15]Mark Satin, *Politics*, p. 98.
[16]Benjamin Creme, *The Reappearance of the Christ and the Masters of Wisdom* (North Hollywood, Calif.: Tara Center, 1980), p. 25.
[17]Shirley MacLaine, *Out on a Limb* (New York: Bantam Books, 1983), p. 45.
[18]David Spangler, *Reflections on the Christ* (Forres, Scotland: Findhorn Publications, 1981), p. 39.

with all humanity and in fact with all life, everywhere, and with the planet as a whole.[19]

The deception is subtle. Kenneth Copeland, though condemning the New Age Cult, may be espousing some hidden New Age thought. He has preached:

> God is God. He is a Spirit. . . . And He imparted in you when you were born again. Peter said it just as plain. He said, "We are partakers of the Divine Nature." That Nature is alive, eternal in absolute perfection, and that was imparted, injected into your spirit man, and you have that imparted into you by God just the same as you imparted into your child the nature of humanity.
>
> That child wasn't born a whale. It was born a human. . . . Well, now, you don't have a human, do you? No, you are one. You don't have a god in you. You *are* one.[20]

Earl Paulk, another Christian preacher, writes the same thing, declaring we are little gods:

> Just as dogs have puppies and cats have kittens, so God has little gods. . . . Until we comprehend that we are little gods and we begin to act like little gods, we cannot manifest the Kingdom of God.[21]

M. Scott Peck, in his book *The Road Less Traveled*, tells us that we are growing toward godhood:

> For no matter how much we may like to pussyfoot around it, all of us who postulate a loving God and really think about it eventually come to a single terrifying idea: God wants us to become Himself (or Herself or Itself). We are growing toward godhood. God is the goal of evolution. It is God who is the source of

[19]Satin, *Politics*, p. 148.
[20]Kenneth Copeland, "The Force of Love," Tape BCC–56.
[21]Earl Paulk, *Satan Unmasked* (K Dimension Publishing, 1984), pp. 96–97.

the evolutionary force and God who is the destination. . . .[22]

Visualization and Guided Imagery

There is a danger that some believers may be led astray by the New Age teaching of visualization, guided imagery. Biblical visualization is meditation on Christ and submission to His direction as revealed in Scripture. But Pastor Cho, the leader of the world's largest Christian church, expressed some ideas bordering on New Age meditation in his book *The Fourth Dimension*:

> We've got to learn how . . . to visualize and dream the answer as being completed as we go to the Lord in prayer. We should always try to visualize the end result as we pray. In that way, with the power of the Holy Spirit, we can incubate that which we want God to do for us. . . .[23]

C. S. Lovett, while advocating meditation, confirms that the visualization he refers to is the same as that used by cults:

> Would it shock you to learn that God's healing power is available through your own mind and you can trigger it by faith! . . . If you had DIRECT ACCESS to your unconscious mind, you could command ANY DISEASE to be healed in a flash. . . . SOUNDS LIKE MIND SCIENCE? I admit that. It's true that the cults have discovered certain of God's healing laws and use them to lure people into their webs. . . . But let me ask, should born-again believers be denied healing simply because certain cults exploit these laws?[24]

Norman Vincent Peale calls visualization (New Age meditation) "positive thinking carried one step further."[25]

But *guided imagery* can open us up to counterfeit Christs

---

[22]M. Scott Peck, *The Road Less Traveled* (New York: Simon and Schuster, 1978), pp. 269–270.

[23]Paul Yonggi Cho, *The Fourth Dimension*, vol. 2 (Logos, 1979), pp. 26–27.

[24]C.S. Lovett, "The Medicine of Your Mind," *Personal Christianity* (August 1979).

[25]Norman Vincent Peale, *Positive Imaging* (Revell, 1982), p. 1.

or angels of light (2 Cor. 11:14). Douglas Groothuis warns:

> An elaborate visualization exercise could induce an altered state of consciousness quite amenable to demonic insurgents. Shakti Gawain, for instance, says that "creative visualization" can easily introduce us to "spirit guides," the likes of which would be thrilled to meet us.[26]

We must also recognize that man's imagination is affected by the Fall. Gen. 6:5 says: "The LORD saw how great man's wickedness on the earth had become, and that every inclination of the thoughts of his heart was only evil all the time." Visualization can be dangerous, but since the New Age movement does not believe in the falleness of man, it becomes especially dangerous.

Positive Confession and Positive Thinking

There is a danger that New Age thought may lead some Christians astray with *positive confession* or *positive thinking*. The danger comes in the form of teaching that says man is a "little god" and thus has the power to speak creatively, bringing good or evil into existence through his word. Positive confession produces "good" and negative confession creates "evil."

Gloria Copeland related her methodology for buying a house she wanted:

> I began to see that I already had authority over that house and authority over the money I needed to purchase it. I said, "In the name of Jesus, I take authority over the money I need. (I called out the specific amount.) I command you to come to me . . . in Jesus' Name. Ministering spirits, you go and cause it to come." . . . (Speaking of angels . . . when you become the voice of God in the earth by putting His Words in your mouth, you put your angels to work! They are highly trained and capable helpers; they know how to get the job done.)[27]

---

[26]Douglas Groothuis, *Confronting the New Age* (Downers Grove: InterVarsity Press, 1988), p. 183.

[27]Gloria Copeland, *God's Will Is Prosperity* (Harrison House, 1978), pp. 48–49.

Dr. Robert Schuller, addressing a large audience of Unity Ministers-in-training, said:

> I believe that the responsibility in this age is to "positivize" religion. Now this probably doesn't have much bearing on you people, being Unity people, you're positive. But I talk a great deal to groups that are not positive . . . even to what we would call Fundamentalists who deal constantly with words like *sin, salvation, repentance, guilt,* and that sort of thing.[28]

Syncretism

There is a danger that New Age thought might cause some believers to develop syncretistic leanings regarding other world religions. This is because New Agers teach that all religions contain the same core truth—man is divine. Matthew Fox, Catholic theologian, was clearly syncretistic in the portion of his writings about "Deep Ecumenism," from which I quoted earlier in this chapter.

The Goddess in Everyone

There is a danger that New Age thought could lead some to make God female, to totally abandon the biblical image of God. The Bible presents God with both feminine and masculine characteristics, but the male imagery is much stronger than the female. Losing sight of this truth would make Him less than He really is, reducing His power and authority and making Him synonymous with the sex goddesses that the Old Testament condemned.

New Age author Matthew Fox writes:

> Religion and culture that represses and distorts the maternal will also repress the ancient tradition of God as Mother and of the goddess in every person. Jesus came to restore that trust to the patriarchal and militaristic culture of his day. . . .

---

[28]Dave Hunt, *The Seduction of Christianity* (Eugene, Ore.: Harvest House), p. 153.

The crucifixion of Jesus was the logical result of his frontal assault on patriarchy.[29]

Eastern Meditation

There is a danger that New Age thought could cause some Christians to transform biblical meditation into Eastern forms of meditation.

One Christian writer proposes meditation in a form that borders on Eastern patterns. He writes:

> In your imagination allow your spiritual body, shining with light, to rise out of your physical body . . . up through the clouds and into the stratosphere . . . deeper and deeper into outer space until there is nothing except the warm presence of the eternal Creator.

Abandoning Moral Foundations

There is a danger of New Age thought weakening the moral structure of the Church because moral absolutes are denied by New Agers. All is relative. "Values clarification," a technique many Christian parents are ignorant about, allows people to choose their own moral base from which to make decisions.

Esoteric Christianity

Because of the similarity in terminology, some Christians may be led astray by the teachings of "*Esoteric Christianity*," spiritual wisdom limited to a few knowing elite. This is a New Age mystical reinterpretation of orthodox (Exoteric) Christianity. Douglas Groothuis comments on how the New Age movement views Exoteric Christianity:

> The true gospel of the One is thought to be the esoteric side of Christianity. *Exoteric Christianity* is the Westernized substitute and is barren of spiritual au-

[29]Matthew Fox, *The Coming of the Cosmic Christ* (New York: Harper and Row, 1988), p. 31.

thenticity, expressing what Wilber calls "average-mode mentality." *Esoteric* Christianity is in tune with "the perennial philosophy" of the One which manifests itself in all religious traditions. The New Age Christ stands against orthodox Christianity.[30]

Doctrinal Deviations to Watch for

One of the greatest threats to the Church is doctrinal confusion caused by New Age thought. Since New Agers use many Christian words, confusion seems likely because many Christians are unaware that good words have been radically redefined with bad meanings.

The Doctrine of Revelation

New Agers believe in continuing revelation from God. They believe that "the Word of God [is] revealed in every age and dispensation. In the days of Moses it was the Pentateuch; in the days of Jesus, the Gospel; in the days of Mohammed, the Messenger of God, the Qur'an; in this day, the Bayan.[31]

Benjamin Creme describes the way in which he receives his New Age revelations:

> It descends on me and comes down as far as the solar plexus and a kind of cone is formed, like that, in light. There is an emotional outflow as well. It is the mental overshadowing which produces the rapport so that I can hear, inwardly, the words.[32]

The Nature of God

God is made an impersonal sum of all existence. Benjamin Creme writes:

> God is the sum total of all that exists in the whole of

---

[30]Douglas Groothuis, *Unmasking the New Age* (Downers Grove: InterVarsity Press, 1986), p. 146.
[31]Baha'u'llah, *Gleanings from the Writings of Baha'u'llah* (Wilmette, Ill.: Baha'i Publishing Trust, 1952), p. 270.
[32]Creme, *The Reappearance*, p. 108.

the manifested and unmanifested universe.[33]

Spangler echoes the idea, writing:

> God is a universal consciousness, a universal life, to
> the extent that our finiteness can express him.[34]

The Uniqueness of Jesus Christ

Creme puts Christ among our peers, declaring that Christ
is divine "in exactly the sense that we are divine." But the
same Christ-spirit dwelt in "Hercules, Hermes, Rama, Mithra
. . . Krishna, Buddha, and the Christ." All these were "perfect
men in their time, all sons of men who became Sons of God,
for having revealed their innate Divinity."[35]

Shirley MacLaine tells us Christ was good, but not necessarily divine:

> Christ was the most advanced human ever to walk
> on this planet.[36]

The Difference Between God and Man

God is made the all-encompassing soul of the universe,
and man is made a god because he contains part of god.
Benjamin Creme writes:

> One of the major teachings of the Christ [is] the fact
> of God immanent, immanent in all creation, in man-
> kind and all creation, that there is nothing else but
> God; that we are all part of a great Being.[37]
>
> Man is an emerging god and thus requires the for-
> mation of modes of loving which will allow this God
> to flourish.[38]

---

[33]Ibid., p. 115.
[34]David Spangler, *Anthology* (Forres, Scotland: Findhorn Publications, 1978), p. 83.
[35]Creme, *The Reappearance*, pp. 115, 28.
[36]MacLaine, *Out on a Limb*, p. 91.
[37]Creme, *The Reappearance*, p. 134.
[38]Benjamin Creme, *Messages from Maitreya the Christ* (Los Angeles: Tara Press, 1980), p. 170.

Sin and Salvation

The need for sacrifice and atonement, a cultural universal, is seen by the New Age as an outdated remnant of Jewish thought. Benjamin Creme rejects orthodox Christianity because it presents "a picture of the Christ impossible for the majority of thinking people today to accept as the One and Only son of God, sacrificed by His Loving Father to save Humanity from the results of its sins; as a Blood Sacrifice straight out of the old and outworn Jewish Dispensation."[39]

David Spangler writes that "man is his own Satan just as man is his own salvation."[40]

The Doctrine of Resurrection

The resurrection we await is substituted with the ongoing cycle of reincarnation in the New Age. James Sire writes:

> Reincarnation is the successive embodiment of the soul in a series of different mortal bodies; resurrection is the transformation of a person's own mortal body to an immortal one.[41]

Groothuis contrasts the two:

> Reincarnation is thought to be an ongoing process, whereas resurrection is a one-time and final event. Moreover, the sovereign Lord is in control of the time and type of resurrection; whereas an impersonal law of karma or the discarnate soul itself is the active agent in the case of reincarnation.[42]

---

[39]Creme, *The Reappearance*, p. 25.
[40]Spangler, *Reflections on the Christ*, p. 39.
[41]James Sire, *Scripture Twisting* (Downers Grove: InterVarsity, 1980), p. 92.
[42]Groothuis, *Confronting*, p. 95.

Chapter 7

Reincarnation and the New Age

One of the key teachings of the New Age movement, a doctrine virtually essential to its entire concept of "salvation," is the doctrine of transmigration of the soul—or as it is popularly known in the Western world, *reincarnation*. It is not within the scope of this volume to give an exhaustive refutation of this concept. Norman Geisler, Robert Morey, and other good researchers have competently refuted reincarnation in detail; but I cannot write about the New Age without discussing it.

Various surveys taken across the United States in the last twenty years have indicated that Americans have progressively become sensitive and even friendly to the idea of reincarnation. This can be traced directly to the penetration of our culture by Hinduism and other religions that have exerted a powerful influence. The latest survey on reincarnation indicates more than 58 percent of Americans polled either believed in it or believed it to be a distinct possibility.

The New Age movement, as we have noted, relies heavily on the concept of cyclic rebirth operating according to the

law of karma (what you sow you reap in identical propor-
tions). Justice is satisfied in that no matter how long it takes
and how many successive reincarnations are necessary, a person keeps on paying for his misdeeds until his "bad karma
has been balanced by good karma."

The noted New Age writer Marilyn Ferguson cites reincarnation as one of the pillars of the New Age movement;
and in the *Aquarian Gospel of Jesus the Christ,* a New Age publication, we are told that the Lord Jesus himself taught reincarnation after learning it from the yogis of India. We are
also told that dishonest church theologians and church councils removed the teaching of reincarnation from both the Old
and the New Testament, but now the New Age movement is
restoring it to its proper prominence.

The Church Universal and Triumphant, which is headed
by Elizabeth Clare Prophet, has published an entire volume
dealing with the allegedly hidden years of Jesus and the secret
teachings that He transmitted to His disciples, but which were
censored by later ecclesiastical powers.

We at the Christian Research Institute have reviewed this
work and found the lack of genuine scholarship appalling,
not to mention the detailed inaccuracies and misinterpreta-
tions of scriptures and other bona-fide historical sources. It
makes an argument from silence that falls by its own weight.

It is sufficient to point out that not a single shred of evidence exists that reincarnation was part of the theology of
either the Old or the New Testament. This and the fact that
we can reproduce over 90 percent of the New Testament
from known manuscript sources from existing quotations of
the Church Fathers during the first four centuries establish
the reliability of the text. There simply is no evidence that
any councils tampered with the text of the Scriptures.

Reincarnation and the Bible

The following biblical passages are often cited by advocates of reincarnation in order to substantiate their views.
Though not all reincarnationists utilize the same biblical pas-

sages as proof texts, those verses that I quote are consistently cited in almost every book I have read on the subject.

Old Testament Passages

> *Naked came I out of my mother's womb, and naked shall I return thither.* (Job 1:21)

Reincarnationists argue that Job was implying a future return to his mother's womb to be reborn.

Christian Response: A proper understanding of the Old Testament concept of the womb is quite revealing. The Hebrews equated the womb with the dust of the earth (Gen. 3:19). They reasoned that just as man came from the dust of the earth in creation, so he would return to the dust in death. An illustration of this is seen clearly in Ps. 139:13–15 where "womb" and "depths of the earth" are equated. Therefore, the context of Job's statement had to do with the destiny of the body at death, its final decay and disintegration into the dust from which it had come, *not* with some future incarnation.

> *The Lord possessed me in the beginning of his way, before his works of old. . . . I was set up from everlasting, from the beginning, or ever the earth was. . . . Before the hills was I brought forth. . . . When he prepared the heavens, I was there. . . . When he appointed the foundations of the earth: Then I was by him, as one brought up with him: and I was daily his delight, rejoicing always before him.* (Prov. 8:22–31)

Reincarnationists argue that these passages refer to the preexistence of the soul and, therefore, an obvious allusion to preincarnate souls awaiting rebirth.

Christian Response: First, the preexistence of the soul does not prove that reincarnation is true. Second, it does not necessarily follow that belief in the preexistence of the soul demands belief in reincarnation. By arguing in this manner, reincarnationists assume what they are trying to prove. Third, the *context* of Proverbs 8 is not referring to the literal preexistence of souls or reincarnation. Rather, the context is referring to the Wisdom of God as having existed from all eternity as a guide to those who seek such from the Lord. Furthermore (and most modern commentaries will bare this out), the writer of Proverbs is communicating (in Hebrew poetry) a personified Wisdom older than the creation—something the Jewish mind clearly understood.

> *Then the word of the Lord came unto me, saying, Before I formed thee in the belly I knew thee; and before thou camest forth out of the womb I sanctified thee.* . . . (Jer. 1:4–5)

Those who believe in reincarnation say this passage proves that God literally knew individuals before they were born. Hence, Jeremiah had lived before.

Christian Response: The context of the passage indicates that God was referring not to Jeremiah's past life or literal preexistence but to God's *foreknowledge* and *calling* of Jeremiah as a prophet to the nations before he was ever born. In other words, Jeremiah's calling and birth existed in the mind of God before they actually transpired. Furthermore, the foreknowledge of God is a theme that is not uncommon through the Old and New Testaments. (See: Isa. 46:9–10; Gal. 1:15; and Rom. 4:17.) Since God is omniscient, having knowledge of all events (past, present, and future), it would logically follow that He could speak of individuals or events that were not yet physically a reality. Paul confirms this in Romans 4 when he notes that God "calleth those things which be not as though they were" (4:17).

New Testament Passages

> *And if you are willing to accept it, he [John the Baptist] is the Elijah who was to come.* (Matt. 11:7–14, NIV)

Reincarnationists claim Jesus was clearly stating that John the Baptist was the reincarnation of the prophet Elijah.

Christian Response: The argument that John the Baptist was a reincarnation of Elijah can be diffused by simply pointing out that the role or ministry of John the Baptist was "in the spirit and power" of Elijah's ministry (Luke 1:17). The text nowhere states that John the Baptist was literally Elijah reincarnated. The fact is that John the Baptist, when asked whether he was Elijah, denied it (John 1:21). Jesus was simply stating that John the Baptist was fulfilling *functionally* and *prophetically*, the ministry of the prophet Elijah as the "voice of the one crying in the wilderness."

> *And Jesus went out, and his disciples, into the towns of Cesarea Philippi: and by the way he asked his disciples, saying unto them, Whom do men say that I am? And they answered, John the Baptist: but some say, Elias; and others, One of the prophets. And he saith unto them, But whom say ye that I am?* (Mark 8:27–30)

The reincarnationist assumes that by asking His disciples to identify Him, Jesus was intentionally inferring that He had lived before.

Christian Response: While it is true that others were mistaken concerning Jesus' identity, the disciples (specifically Peter) correctly identified Him as the Christ, the Messiah (v. 30). Jesus affirms Peter's confession by warning them all not to tell anyone about His identity at that time. Therefore, far from inferring reincarnation, both Peter and Jesus agree: He (Jesus) was the Messiah of Jewish hope, the fulfillment of the prophetic scriptures.

> *Jesus answered and said unto him, Verily, verily, I say to thee, Except a man be born again, he cannot see the kingdom of God.* (John 3:3)

Reincarnationists argue that Jesus was referring to cyclic rebirth when He said that one must be born again.

Christian Response: The context of John 3:1–12 is clearly referring to spiritual rebirth, not physical rebirth. Jesus made that point in verse six when He said, "That which is born of the flesh is flesh, and that which is born of the Spirit is spirit." Furthermore, the phrase "born again" is often translated "born from above," keeping true to the original language. Implicit in this statement is the biblical doctrine of regeneration or conversion, an event that takes place only once and has nothing remotely to do with cyclic rebirth. Peter states the same thought when he wrote: "Being born again, not of corruptible seed, but of incorruptible, by the word of God, which liveth and abideth for ever" (1 Pet. 1:23).

> *And as Jesus passed by, he saw a man which was blind from his birth. And his disciples asked him, saying, Master, who did sin, this man, or his parents, that he was born blind?* (John 9:1–2)

Reincarnationists believe this man was born blind because of the wrongdoing that he had committed in his previous life—an obvious reference to the law of karma.

Christian Response: The argument is quickly refuted by reading further in the text. Verse three reads, "Jesus answered, Neither hath this man sinned, nor his parents: but that the works of God should be made manifest in him." Had this been a situation involving bad karma, Jesus clearly would not have said what He did, nor would He have healed the man of his infirmity. Reincarnational theology forbids one from interfering with another man's karma.

> *For this Melchizedek, king of Salem . . . which is, King of peace; without father, without mother, without descent, having neither beginning of days, nor end of life; but made like unto the Son of God. . . .* (Heb. 7:1–3)

The reincarnationist argues that Melchizedek was an earlier incarnation of Jesus Christ.

Christian Response: Though the details of Melchizedek's life are somewhat sketchy, most commentaries point out that he was a prototype, or model, of Christ who was to come. He is called a man and could not have been Christ because there was only one incarnation (See: John 1:1, 14, 18). Furthermore, even a cursory reading of Hebrews 7 will point out that Christ is a high priest "after the order" or according to the likeness of Melchizedek, *not* that He was Melchizedek in a former life.

Arguments for Past-Life Recall

Advocates of reincarnation argue that reincarnation is true because many people have experienced *past-life recall*. Past-life recall experiences fall into several categories. Four main types are (1) intuitive recall, (2) spontaneous recall, (3) psychic recall, and (4) hypnotic regression.

Intuitive Recall

Intuitive recall or deja vu is the experience of a feeling or strong impression that one has seen the same thing before or met someone before even though the person may be seeing something or meeting someone for the first time. Reincarnationists argue that this is an indication that one has actually met that person or visited that place before in a past life.

Christian Response: Intuitive recall can be explained by pointing out that when a person feels that he has been somewhere before or thinks that he has met that person before, he is simply experiencing an attempt by the subconscious mind to relate the present experience to something in the past. For instance, a person may have seen a picture or photograph of that person or place and, although he can't consciously remember seeing it, his subconscious mind relates the encounter to the picture or photograph, causing that person to think that he has been there before or met that person in a previous life.

Spontaneous Recall

Spontaneous recall usually, but not always, occurs in children who insist that they are someone else who lived in a previous life. Reincarnationists argue that some of these cases have been scientifically verified and are, therefore, irrefutable.

Christian Response: Despite reincarnationist claims, those cases involving children claiming to be someone else who lived before have not been scientifically verified. In fact, the majority of documented cases that seem to exhibit genuine features of supposed past lives are explained by one of the following: (1) conscious or unconscious fraud, (2) cryptomnesia, (3) genetic memory, or (4) spirit communication. Satan would be interested in contradicting the scriptures which flatly state that we live one life (Heb. 9:27).

Psychic Recall

Psychic recall is remembering past lives through seances, mediums, or ESP experiments. Reincarnationists argue that since knowledge acquired through these means is supernatural, it must, therefore, be true.

Christian Response: Information acquired through occultic means will not lead a person to truth but into error. Though the experience may be real, or even supernatural, if it is not grounded in truth, it will lead one into further deception. Information acquired through seances, mediums, or ESP experiments is occultic in nature and therefore fraudulent. Since the Bible teaches that participation in any occult activity is forbidden (Ex. 22:18; Lev. 19:31; Deut. 13:1–5), and that the real power behind these practices is satanic and evil, those who seek to validate their experiences through such means are being tricked into believing that they have lived before.

Hypnotic Regression

Hypnotic regression is the recall of past lives through hypnosis. Reincarnationists argue that if a person remembers his past life under hypnosis, then the person must have experienced it.

Christian Response: This is the most popular argument given to support past-life recall, but it is still under suspicion by many professional hypnotists. The nature of the hypnotic state is still largely unknown. Further, the subject is highly susceptible to suggestions and other mental or psycho-spiritual transmissions, and therefore unreliable. Those cases that involve hypnotic regression are deriving their information from memories of the subconscious mind or from genuine occultic sources. Neither case is sufficient to prove that reincarnation is true.

The Hopeless Salvation of Reincarnation

As we read the multiple references by New Age writers to reincarnation and karma, we see one thread running through virtually all of them. The purpose of reincarnation is to, in effect, atone for misdeeds (*personal sins* in the Christian context). Each rebirth in the reincarnational wheel of life provides the opportunity to correct the errors of past lives so that final redemption or absorption of the soul into the divine world soul (Nirvana) removes any necessity for a savior from sin.

We become our own saviors. The doctrine of reincarnation is a subtle and masked attack against the salvation that Jesus Christ purchased for the Church on the cross. The writer of Hebrews declares:

> For Christ did not enter a man-made sanctuary that was only a copy of the true one; he entered heaven itself, now to appear for us in God's presence. Nor did he enter heaven to offer himself again and again, the way the high priest enters the Most Holy Place every year with blood that is not his own. Then Christ would have had to suffer many times since the creation of the world. But now he has appeared once for all at the end of the ages to do away with sin by the sacrifice of himself.
>
> Just as man is destined to die once, and after that to face judgment, so Christ was sacrificed once to take away the sins of many people; and he will appear a second time, not to bear sin, but to bring salvation to those who are waiting for him. (Heb. 9:24–28, NIV)

We are also reminded that with "one offering he hath perfected for ever them that are sanctified" (Heb. 10:14). The writer of Hebrews does not fail to remind us repeatedly that Christ "by himself purged our sins, sat down on the right hand of the majesty on high" (Heb. 1:3).

The figure of the suffering servant portrayed in Isaiah 53 and fulfilled on Calvary when the Lord Jesus cried "it is finished" is a total stranger to the reincarnationist. And just as they do not need Christ to die for their sins, they do not need to accept His resurrection from the dead to seal the covenant of divine redemption. Reincarnation in the New Age Cult is a means of circumventing the cross and replacing our resurrection, not with an immortal or glorified body, as the Apostle Paul teaches us in 1 Corinthians 15, but with an endless procession of corruptible bodies in which we must attempt to work out our final salvation by the law of karma.

It should never be forgotten that in biblical theology, salvation is the gift of God (Rom. 6:23), and if the gift is rejected it is followed by the judgment. Reincarnation contradicts apostolic authority and the direct teaching of Christ himself. Jesus said, prophesying of His bodily resurrection from the dead, "Destroy this temple and in three days I will raise it up." John reminds us that Jesus was speaking of "the temple of his body" (John 2:19–21).

The God of the Bible sealed the validity of the covenant He had made with man through His Son by raising Christ from the dead, and without this there is no validity to Christianity. This is a fact Satan knows only too well, hence the substitution of reincarnation for salvation and resurrection.

We are appointed to die "once," but the reincarnationist in his teaching is appointed to die almost endlessly, and in the end to no avail. How true the words of Scripture ring, "For by grace are saved through faith; and that not by yourselves: it is the gift of God: not works [i.e., karma], lest any man should boast" (Eph. 2:8–9).

The Bible repeatedly warns of judgment for sin after the death of the body. We are told in 2 Pet. 2:9: "The Lord knoweth how to deliver the godly out of temptations, and to reserve the unjust unto the day of judgment to be punished." We should further observe that judgment is an event (Acts 17:31), not an endless cycle.

The New Age Cult becomes a victim of its own theology; it cannot break out of the circle of karma, therefore its concept of redemption is illusory. The Prince of Life breaks all such cycles of slavery, for He alone can say, "I am the resurrection, and the life: he that believeth in me, though he were dead, yet shall he live: and whosoever liveth and believeth in me shall never die" (John 11:25–26). Jesus Christ promised in the triumphal glory of His own resurrection, "Because I live, ye shall live also" (John 14:19).

The words of Christ flow like pure oxygen into the polluted muddle of reincarnational theology. They ever remind us that one day Jesus will raise up those who put their faith in Him (John 6:40), *not* in their own abilities to atone for their sins by human efforts. We have been begotten by God to "a living hope through the resurrection of Jesus Christ from the dead," and it is more than significant that those who teach reincarnation not only do not rise from the dead, but that they have simply never known the life of God nor His forgiveness (1 Pet. 1:3, NIV; John 3:36).

The Agony of Error

Reincarnation cannot answer practical questions. It cannot come to grips with the fact that, while it has been talking about doing good for mankind, tens of millions of people have starved and suffered and endured horrible persecutions under India's caste system simply because reincarnation held them in a particular caste, cycle after cycle, so that it was impossible for them to ever escape. Even today in India and in other lands, people who believe this doctrine allow their children to starve while rats and sacred cows live. What kind of reflection is this of the God who said, "Let the little children come to me, and do not hinder them, for the kingdom of heaven belongs to such as these"? (Matt. 19:14, NIV).

Reincarnation does away with the dignity of man by reducing him to an impersonal origin. Instead of being a unique image of God, we find ourselves nothing more than a single stage in a constant cycle repeated from eon to eon, finding neither rest nor peace. For those who believe in reincarnation, the gospel of Jesus Christ speaks forcefully and persuasively: "Come unto me, all ye that labour and are heavy laden, and I will give you rest. Take my yoke upon you, and learn of me; for I am meek and lowly in heart: and ye shall find rest unto your souls" (Matt. 11:28–29).

Chapter 8

Christian Confrontation With New Agers

The practical side of learning about New Age occultic and cultic theology and those who have become its victims is to encounter them with the stark contrast between historic Christian theology and New Age beliefs. But in order to do this effectively, there are certain steps that must be taken and methods that must be applied to insure maximum exposure and penetration of Christian evangelism and apologetics.

The Christian will learn almost immediately that after he witnesses to the truthfulness of the gospel message, he will have to introduce Christian apologetics, a reasoned defense of the validity of Christian truth.

Though some disagree with the need for the two-pronged approach, I have been successfully walking the line between evangelism and apologetics for over thirty-eight years. It is by no means an easy task, but from my own experience and study, I include the following suggestions. They can be extremely helpful, allowing you to get beyond the basics without the error of becoming a master of the obvious.

The Preparation of Prayer

The Apostle John reminds us that "if we ask any thing according to his will, he heareth us: and if we know that he hear us, whatsoever we ask, we know that we have the petitions that we desired of him" (1 John 5:14–15). Since we know this to be true and that His will is that everyone be saved (2 Pet. 3:9), we must pray before we encounter the person we have been led to confront, continue to pray while we are speaking with them, and pray more after the confrontation. It must be specific prayer, calling to mind the promises that God has made, and asking Him to open the eyes and ears of the soul and mind of that person. We want the glorious light of the gospel of Christ, who is the image of God, to penetrate what is most assuredly spiritual and mental darkness. The Apostle Paul said:

> But if our gospel be hid, it is hid to them that are lost: in whom the god of this world hath blinded the minds of them which believe not, lest the light of the glorious gospel of Christ, who is the image of God, should shine unto them. (2 Cor. 4:4–5)

This should not surprise us because the Scriptures are clear in stating that "the natural man receiveth not the things of the Spirit of God: for they are foolishness unto him: neither can he know them, because they are spiritually discerned" (1 Cor. 2:14).

We know, then, that if we are praying for God to open the eyes and ears of their minds and of their spiritual natures, our prayers are in accordance with His will. We are to plant the seed of scriptural truth just as the proverbial sower did, ever watering it with prayer, confident that "he which hath begun a good work in you will perform it until the day of Jesus Christ" (Phil. 1:6).

Repeat and Reword

We must cultivate with consistency the spiritual fruit of patience, and learn to state our position at least three times in different words (a dictionary of synonyms is very helpful here). People frequently simply do not "hear" the first time, but need the reinforcement of repetition. Should you find yourself losing patience, simply remember how difficult it was for you to accept the truth of the gospel when you were in the same condition as the person you are talking with. Pray that the Lord would multiply this fruit during your time of encounter.

Communicate Your Love

Whenever possible, communicate your spiritual concern for the person, citing Lev. 19:18 as your motive and go beyond the desire to make a statistic out of the person for some local congregation. New Agers are particularly sensitive to sincere love and concern for their well-being. Love demonstrates that concern. Medieval theologians had a saying: "The love of God conquers all things." Remember, the Lord would never have commanded us to love our neighbor as ourself if we did not have the capacity to do so. If you pray for this, it will manifest itself to that person.

Seek Common Ground

Find a common ground from which you can approach the controversial issues—perhaps from his religious background, his family, or certain goals or practices that you have in common with him. You might discuss abortion, Rotary, ecology, or patriotism. Whatever helps establish an amicable relationship facilitates communication, particularly if it is in the realm of spiritual values.

Define Terminology

Define your terminology in an inoffensive way, and when he is talking about God, love, Jesus Christ, salvation, or reincarnation, ask him to explain what he means. Try to arrive at a dictionary definition rather than a subjective judgment. There is a formidable difference between a dictionary definition and an encyclopedia of subjective comments. We can *communicate* with properly defined words in a context of objective truth, but a "feeling" about what a term means says nothing.

Be sure that you yourself are familiar with definitions, particularly when you get to the special terminology redefined by the cults and occult. These red-flag words can be easily defused with a dictionary reference. This is particularly true when it comes to such subjects as the nature of man, human sin, the problem of evil, and divine judgment or justice. Take care to keep the definitions simple.

Dr. Donald Grey Barnhouse once compared the communication of the gospel to feeding cows. He said, "Get the hay down out of the loft onto the barn floor where the cows can get at it." Keep it as simple as possible. You are not there to impress the person with how much you know or how articulate you can be. You are there to be a representative of the Holy Spirit, whose task it is to "reprove the world of sin, and of righteousness, and of judgment" (John 16:8).

God has not called us to convert the world; God has called us to plant the seeds of the gospel and water them with prayer. It is the task of the Spirit to bring those seeds to life, and He has promised that if we are faithful, He will.

Question, Don't Teach

Do not try to teach a New Ager or cultist, for the moment you don the teacher's garment, he will "tune out" just as he has been programmed to do. When the Lord Jesus Christ was teaching during His earthly ministry, He reasoned with people and consistently asked questions. When they could not answer what He had to say, then He began to teach them. His dialogue was more successful than if He had begun teaching.

People are threatened by others who intimidate them with a professorial attitude that communicates an air of superiority, whether it is real or imagined. However, because our manner may be interpreted as haughtiness, the watchword is caution.

Jesus questioned the Pharisees, the Sadducees, the scribes, the Herodians, and even common men on subjects for which they had no real answers of enduring value. If incarnate Truth was that tactful, we could use a little sanctified tact ourselves. Jesus' encounter with the woman at the well (John 4) was a good illustration of our Lord's techniques, and the Holy Spirit thought it important enough to record so that we might profit from the Lord's knowledge of human nature.

Read the Word

Wherever possible, use your Bible and ask the New Ager to read the specific passages under discussion. I call this technique "falling on the sword." Since the Bible is called the sword of the Spirit (Eph. 6), we need only position the sword properly as they read and it will penetrate, even where all of our arguments and reasoning have failed.

The Bible reminds us again and again that "the Word of God is not bound" (2 Tim. 2:9), but it is "quick, and powerful, and sharper than a two-edged sword, piercing even to the dividing asunder of the soul and the spirit, and the joints and marrow, and is a discerner of the thoughts and intents of the heart" (Heb. 4:12). You must consistently bring the New Ager back to the authority of what God has said, particularly in regard to the consciousness of personal sin.

Do not attack the New Ager with the sword of the Spirit, but rather permit the Spirit to use *His* instrument to cut through the scar tissue that sin has created on the minds and spirits of unregenerate men. The Spirit is the master teacher and the greatest of all surgeons, let Him do the work. You must simply prepare the patient for surgery.

Avoid Criticism

Avoid attacking New Age cult leaders or founders of specific groups, for even if the New Ager knows that you are correct, he remains true to human nature and defends against what he considers to be unloving criticism. The New Ager is unaware that revealing truth is the most loving thing a person can do, but that truth must be spoken in love, and then only after much work has been done on your part to show that you speak not out of bitterness or an accusatory spirit, but simply from the perspective of historical fact.

Commend

Praise the zeal, dedication, and (wherever possible) the goals of the New Age movement, because its basic nature is both messianic and millennial. The New Age Cult is seeking the right things, but with the wrong methods and with wrong reasons, sometimes merely because their vision is impaired by sin. Remind them that their quest for an end to poverty, disease, suffering, racial discrimination, inequalities, and economic and political tyranny are things with which Christianity has been concerned for almost two millennia.

Many New Agers are genuinely seeking millennial conditions on the earth. But there will be no kingdom without the King, no love without justice, and no power without control. Point out to them from the Scriptures that those who follow Jesus Christ will inherit all these things as a *gift* from God and that the kingdoms of this world, when they become the kingdoms of our Lord and of His Christ, will reflect many of the values they now profess to hold sacred.

Take time to laud them for their efforts in the area of conservation and concern for the well-being of the planet as well as the creatures that live on it. Impress upon them your concern in these same areas, but use the opportunity to point out that no matter how hard we work, we still live in a world that is suffering from irremedial conditions caused by man's rebellion against his Creator.

Cite a few of the imperfections that demonstrate that fact: war, the oppression of minorities, and the abuse of human rights. These are all reminders of the fact that "all have sinned and come short of the glory of God" (Rom. 3:23).

New Agers are sometimes disarmed by commendations because they have been incorrectly taught to believe that Christianity is so heavenly minded that it is of no earthly good and that the God of the Bible doesn't care about His creation. Let them see that you understand and that you care. Show that you care because God has shown us His concern in His Word.

Study the New Age

When dealing with New Age thinking, be sure that you can accurately cite New Age leaders and writings. If you do not understand or have not read what your opponent is talking about, make it a point to check it out before you check back with him. This will show him that you are consistent and interested in his well-being and truth as a whole. Be prepared to say, "Well I haven't seen or read that, but I certainly would like to look into it." Then do so.

Define "Jesus"

Ask the New Age believer if he can explain the difference between the Jesus found in the Bible and the Jesus who appears in New Age literature. Take him to 2 Corinthians 11 and pay particular attention to verses three and four:

> But I am afraid that just as Eve was deceived by the serpent's cunning, your minds may somehow be led astray from your sincere and pure devotion to Christ. For if someone comes to you and preaches a Jesus other than the Jesus we preached, or if you receive a different spirit from the one you received, or a different gospel from the one you accepted, you put up with it easily enough.

Let him see that the name "Jesus" means nothing unless it is defined within the context of New Testament revelation.

We can say anything we choose about Jesus, but an accurate portrayal of Him requires facts from the source documents, not from someone attempting to "restore" the "historical Jesus" hundreds or almost two thousand years later when in fact the only historical Jesus is the Jesus of the New Testament.

It is always helpful to show that the word "Jesus" is defined by the New Age completely different than the context of history demands. Use the opportunity to exalt the Lord Jesus Christ, not as one of many messengers sent for a specific period in time for a specific set of needs, but rather as the Lord of the ages, *the* way to God, the embodiment of truth, and the incarnation of life itself.

Let the New Ager understand that his view of Christ as merely an avatar, a messenger of God, is inconsistent with what Jesus said of himself and what the Church has believed. (At that juncture John 3:16–17 can be very helpful if you can read it with them.)

Reveal the Weakness of Moral Relativism

By asking questions, show the New Ager how logically flawed it is to allow subjectivism and moral relativism to lead him. Help him understand that he cannot live consistently with these principles. For instance, ask, "If your truth is your truth and my truth is my truth, how can we be certain about anything? Let us say that my truth happens to be that Einstein was wrong in the theory of relativity and the unified field theories, whereas you and objective truth in both mathematics and physics confirm that he was right. Does it make any difference whether the truth is based on facts or subjective feelings? Was Einstein wrong because I think he was wrong?" Relativism produces no truth.

A good method at this juncture is to point out what the great philosopher Mortimer J. Adler of the University of Chicago said concerning subjective "truth." Dr. Adler wisely observed that the Nazis' argument for killing Jews was a position that could not be refuted in a world of relative morality and ethics. Who could condemn Hitler for murdering six million Jews if their extinction was "his truth." To argue that he was wrong, if you are a relativist, is fallacious because your own definition of truth entitles Hitler as much right to his view as you to yours.

But right and wrong are not determined by voice vote or social criteria; they are founded in abiding standards recognized universally as true—rightly designated as "moral absolutes." You can point out to the New Ager that speeding down Broadway in New York City at ninety miles an hour and failing to be influenced by red, yellow, or green traffic lights merely because he believes them to be irrelevant to the goal of reaching his destination on time will allow him to confront the objective truth that his action constitutes reckless driving when the police arrest him.

Show the Bible to Be Reliable

It is important to set forth the historic reliability of the Bible when discussing the concept of absolute truth with New Agers. The Bible must be seen as a guide to truth superior to those with no credentials whatsoever. We can benefit from a study of biblical history and archeology to add credibility to our position. There are many excellent books on these subjects designed for the pastor and the layman.*

Reveal the Inconsistency of the New Age World View

Point out the underlying differences between Christian and New Age world views and show that the Christian world view is radically more consistent with the world and mankind as we find them.

The world view of the New Age movement is a monistic pantheistic concept. Monistic pantheism, as noted previously, teaches that all is one and all is divine. It makes no division between God and His creation. This is inconsistent with logic and experience since billions of people can speak the personal pronoun "I" from the context of their own experience and lives. Each person is different from all the rest of his fellow-men. Mankind cannot even collectively account for the earth, life, or the problem of evil apart from divine revelation.

I was once talking to a New Age talk show host who, when I quoted Descartes' famous proof "I think, therefore I am," said, "Descartes was obviously mistaken. What he should have said is 'I think I think, therefore I think I am.'"

I replied, "It sounds good, but I can refute that in thirty

---

*See particularly *Evidence That Demands a Verdict* by Josh McDowell.

seconds if you don't interrupt me."

He promised, "I won't interrupt you, but you're not gonna *hit* me to prove that I'm here, are you?"

We both laughed and I assured him that no violence would ensue.

He looked at his wristwatch and said, "Go for it."

"I have been carrying on a conversation with you for about fifteen minutes, have I not?" He looked at me in silence. "If you say that I have not been carrying on a conversation with you, and you have not been carrying on a conversation with me, then one of us is insane and people who talk to people that aren't there are not here very long."

He thought for a moment, then said, "That's a good point but truth is really as each of us perceives it."

I couldn't resist the argument Dr. Adler had made, so I said, "I'm glad to see that you agree with Adolf Hitler in his destruction of the Jews."

He recoiled in horror, but under the pressure of Dr. Adler's argument admitted vigorously that Hitler was wrong, that his perception was wrong. Yet the host, remaining consistent with his philosophy, could find no way to condemn Hitler. He concluded, "I've become illogical in the framework of my own views and must abhor as evil what Hitler did."

The New Age world view simply doesn't work in the hard, nitty-gritty world of everyday experience. It requires ideal conditions to find a place in the mind of the individual and in the events surrounding his life from day to day. Without this, it disintegrates under the hammer blows of sin and circumstances.

We must never allow ourselves to forget that God has planted three things in the minds of all men according to Romans 1. He has made us conscious of His existence as Creator, and it makes us uncomfortable. We are imbued with a conscience that constantly reveals the choices before us as good or evil. And He has made our spirits aware that since there is not perfect justice in this world, judgment must surely come from another one. Descartes called these "innate ideas," but they are actually imparted spiritual concepts that are part of our creation in the image and likeness of God (Gen. 1:26–

27). The words of St. Augustine ring ever true: "Thou has made us, O Lord, and we are thine and our souls are restless until they rest in Thee."

Provide Books or Tapes

Refer the New Ager to some good Christian books, tapes, video cassettes, audio cassettes, booklets, or tracts addressing New Age thinking (or you might give him one). If it is possible, find one that you think communicates effectively and fairly, and tell him that you hope he will seriously consider another point of view and pray about it, because God has promised, "You will seek me and find me when you seek me with all your heart" (Jer. 29:13, NIV).

A Note of Warning

As we think about encountering or confronting people in the New Age Cult, we ought to remember that Christians sometimes can be influenced and even led astray by New Age thinking. John Weldon and John Ankerberg have written:

> Christians are being influenced by the New Age Movement (NAM) principally because of ignorance of biblical teachings and lack of doctrinal knowledge. Because of America's emphasis on materialism, commitment to Christ as Lord in every area of life is sadly lacking. This brings disastrous results. Unfortunately there are Christians who love "the praise of men more than the praise of God" (John 12:43), who integrate the world's ways with their Christian faith (James 1:27; 1 John 2:15; 4:4), or who are ignorant of the extent of spiritual warfare (Acts 20:28–34; 2 Cor. 4:4; Eph. 6:11–23; 2 Pet. 2:1; 1 John 4:1–3).
>
> These sins of American Christianity open us to false philosophy such as the NAM. There are always some Christians who will actively embrace their culture. Whether they attempt to learn from it intellectually or borrow from it spiritually, or relish the enjoyment of worldly pleasures and pastimes, or attempt some kind

of social reform along nominal Christian lines, the result is that their Christian faith becomes diluted or absorbed by an initially appealing but alien culture. This means that to the extent America turns to the New Age, to some degree there will be Christians who will adopt New Age practices or beliefs.[1]

In dealing with the New Age Cult, we are in reality dealing with spiritual warfare against the forces of darkness, and we are told by God to put on the whole armor of heaven so that we will be able to withstand the forces of Satan (Eph. 6:11).

There is no substitute in this conflict for knowledge of the Word of God and the proper use of the sword of the Spirit and the shield of faith to deflect all the flaming arrows of the evil one. The forces arrayed against us are great, the stakes are high: the souls of millions of people. But the promise of God stands sure, we can "overcome them: because greater is he that is in you, than he that is in the world" (1 John 4:4).

Prepare yourself for spiritual combat, study and show yourself approved by God, a workman who won't need to blush with embarrassment, rightly interpreting the word of truth. And above all, lift the shield of faith declaring, "Jesus Christ is Lord to the glory of God the Father." The Christian Church looks to that glorious moment when "the Sun of righteousness will arise with healing in his wings" (Mal. 4:2), and the former things of the cursed earth will pass away and God will make all things new.

This is our blessed hope, the appearing of the glory of the great God and of our Savior Jesus Christ—this is the hope of the Church. This is the hope of the ages.

---

[1]John Ankerberg and John Weldon, *The Facts on the New Age Movement*, p. 22.

Chapter 9

Identifying New Age Groups and Leaders

One of the problems with understanding the New Age Cult is that identifying New Age organizations and leaders is difficult. It is not easy for the average Christian to confront New Agers, but not to know who they are and through which groups and persons they communicate complicates the problem enormously.

The important question is: What are some criteria Christians can use to determine if a group is part of the New Age?

Conclusive Evidence of New Age Thinking

1. The group is openly committed to furthering the New Age (i.e., Age of Aquarius).

2. The group openly espouses distinctively New Age beliefs such as monism ("all is One"), pantheism ("all is God"), gnosticism (salvation or spiritual healing come through special experiences of enlightenment), karma and reincarnation, spiritual evolution, ascended masters (equal with Christ), etc.

3. The group openly advocates New Age/occult practices

such as channeling/mediumship, astrology, psychic healing, numerology, magic, various methods for inducing altered states of consciousness (e.g., meditation, chanting, sensory deprivation, hypnosis, etc.), and the use of crystals or pyramids for psychic reasons.

4. The group uses uniquely New Age terminology such as "create your own reality," "Higher Self," "self-realization," "cosmic consciousness," "universal energy," "chakras," "kundalini," "yin and yang," etc.

Inconclusive Evidence of New Age Thinking

The following criteria are often but not always indicative of New Age involvement. Any red flags raised by these considerations warrant further research but *not* final judgment.

1. The group bases its ideas on questionable assumptions (e.g., humanism, subjectivism, relativism, lack of self-esteem as man's root problem, unlimited human potential).

2. The group practices questionable politics (e.g., it works for or advocates a "new world order" or "planetary guidance system").

3. The group uses New Age phrases (e.g., "new paradigm" or "paradigm shift," "transformation," "self-actualization," "global vision").

4. The group has questionable associations (e.g., ties with or recommends groups such as the Association for Humanistic Psychology, Association for Transpersonal Psychology, Association for Holistic Health, "Green" political parties and movements, Friends of the Earth, Greenpeace, a group such as Est, Lifespring, Silva Mind Control, etc.).

New Age Spokespeople

The following list of New Age spokespersons can help solve the puzzle of whether a group is actually associated with the New Age movement.

Bailey, Alice—Considered by many to be a New Age prophetess. She subscribed to the theosophical doctrine that the spiritual destiny of humanity is guided by Ascended Masters. These Masters are presently working to unfold "the Plan." Bailey also believed Jesus was a "Master" who acted as a bodily vehicle for the Cosmic Christ 2,000 years ago.

Berry, Thomas—A Jesuit theologian whose books promote the idea that there is a sacred element to all that exists. The world view he espouses encourages people to treat all things they encounter as honored and precious manifestations of God.

Besant, Annie—Took over the spiritual leadership of the Theosophical Society when Helena Petrovna Blavatsky died. Wrote two books, *Ancient Wisdom* and *Esoteric Christianity*, which are both still used among New Agers.

Blavatsky, Helena Petrovna—One of the founders of the Theosophical Society. "Theosophy" means "divine wisdom." The goals of Theosophy are to (1) form a universal brotherhood; (2) do comparative study of world religions, science, and philosophy; and (3) explore the psychic and spiritual powers latent in man.

Caddy, Peter and Eileen—Founders of the Findhorn community in the North of Scotland. This community is a prototype New Age learning center. It offers an ongoing educational program in the principles of New Age spirituality and world service.

Capra, Fritjof—Specialist in quantum physics whose books *The Tao of Physics* and *The Turning Point* are popular in New Age circles. In his books he demonstrates the similarities between the emerging holistic world view of physics and mysticism, which, he says, prove interrelatedness of all things in the universe.

Creme, Benjamin—Founder of the Tara Center and author of an important New Age book, *The Reappearance of the Christ and the Masters of Wisdom*. The Tara Center financed full page ads in twenty major newspapers in 1982 announcing "The Christ Is Now Here." Creme, a disciple of Alice Bailey, is popular on the New Age lecture circuit

Ferguson, Marilyn—Author of an important New Age book

entitled *The Aquarian Conspiracy*. Her book explores the ascendancy of a new world view which is receiving its impetus from an underground network set on creating an altogether different society. The society this network is pushing for will be one with an enlarged concept of human potential.

Fox, Matthew—Controversial Catholic theologian whose books are popular among New Agers. He developed a system of thought he calls "Creation Spirituality," a blend of Catholic mysticism, panentheism, environmentalism, and feminism.

Galyean, Beverly—Founder and promoter of "Confluent Education." Her approach involves helping others to see that they are God and that they have the attributes of God. The purpose of human life, says Galyean, is to "reown" the Godlikeness within us.

Keys, Donald—A long-time consultant to United Nation's delegations who founded Planetary Citizens in 1972. Planetary Citizens is dedicated to the transformation of the world through political action.

Knight, J.Z.—A popular New Age channeler who makes regular appearances on TV talk shows. Ramtha, supposedly a thirty-five-thousand-year-old warrior, channels through Ms. Knight and is one of Shirley MacLaine's favorite spirit guides.

Kuhn, Thomas—A scientist whose book *The Structure of Scientific Revolutions* has become very popular among New Agers. The major focus of Kuhn's book is how paradigm shifts occur in the realm of science. New Agers have adapted his theory to describe how paradigm shifts occur in culture.

Lipnack, Jessica—Coauthored *Networking* with Jeffrey Stamps. This book is essentially a catalogue of diverse New Age networks. They point out that networks are autonomous (and hence non-conspiratorial), but often benefit from working together because of their common values and visions.

Lovelock, James—Formulated the "Gaia Hypothesis" and recorded the theory in a book appropriately entitled *Gaia*. "Gaia" is an ancient Greek name for the goddess of the earth. The hypothesis sees the earth and all life on the earth as a single self-supporting organism.

Muller, Robert—A recently retired UN Assistant Secretary General who believes that the human race must transcend all national, linguistic, cultural, racial, and religious differences. He says that we must discover that we are all one big human family.

Mumford, Lewis—Wrote an important book entitled *The Transformations of Man*. The book argues that every transformation human society undergoes rests on a shift in world views. A planetary culture is presently emerging, says Mumford, that will transcend national boundaries and religious differences.

Needleman, Jacob—A popular philosopher in New Age circles, Needleman is considered a pioneer in the development of a "new consciousness." Needleman argues in his books for the need for the esoteric and mystical in Christianity.

Price, John Randolph—Author of *The Planetary Commission*, a book promoting "The World Peace Event" (which was set for December 31, 1986). Price also espouses the idea that Jesus learned to tap into the universal and impersonal "Christ consciousness." He boasts that he too is part of that Christ consciousness. He believes that each human being must look within himself to find his "absolute self" instead of looking to some Christ who is separate from us.

Roberts, Jane—A channeler through whom a spiritual guide named Seth communicated twenty books worth of revelation from the other side.

Roszak, Theodore—A New Age analyst who believes that each person's goal must be to awaken to the god within.

Roszak also says that the idea of a transcendent God who is distinct from the world causes the world to be divested of spiritual significance. Roszak believes that the world of nature has been desacralized by Christianity; it would be much better to recognize God in all things.

Ryerson, Kevin—A New Age channeler who came into prominence because of his affiliation with Shirley MacLaine and her movie "Out on a Limb." Ryerson channels a variety of spirit guides. He believes that the revelations received from such entities are important because of the insights and factual information that has come through them.

Spangler, David—Considered a prophet by many New Agers. Spangler gained fame when he took over the education program at the Findhorn community in Scotland. His two most important books are *Revelation: The Birth of a New Age* and *Reflections on the Christ*.

Stamps, Jeffrey—Coauthored *Networking* with Jessica Lipnack. (See: Lipnack, Jessica.)

Starhawk—A modern Wicca witch who promotes feminist goddess-worship. Starhawk presently works in close association with controversial Catholic theologian Matthew Fox.

Steiner, Rudolf—Founded the Anthroposophical Society in 1924. "Anthroposophy" means "wisdom of man." Steiner taught that people possess the truth within themselves. By cultivating one's occult powers through spiritual exercises, anyone can become a "master of clear vision," thereby gaining extraordinary spiritual insight.

Thompson, William Irwin—Cultural historian who has written several books that trace the emergence of the New Age world view. Thompson believes our world is now moving from "civilization" to "planetization."

Trevelyan, George—A leader of the New Age Movement in Great Britain. His two books, *A Vision of the Aquarian Age and Operation Redemption*, have been well received in New

Age circles. Some of his thinking is similar to Rudolf Steiner. Trevelyan is a popular speaker on the New Age lecture circuit.

Walsh, John—Wrote a book entitled *Intercultural Education in the Community of Man* which became popular among New Agers. The book stresses that the guiding philosophy for an individual's behavior is an awareness of the wholeness of humanity and the interrelatedness and interdependency of all life on planet earth.

New Age Organizations

The following list of organizations includes New Age groups as well as those that, though not definitely New Age, have attracted a following of New Age members.

Association for Humanistic Psychology—A worldwide network that explores human potential, personal growth, and holistic health. The group publishes a journal and features workshops on topics such as optimal health, self-healing, and spirituality.

Association for Research and Enlightenment—This group promotes the teachings of psychic Edgar Cayce. Seminars and workshops are sponsored on topics such as self-hypnosis, visualization, and psychic guidance.

Association for Transpersonal Psychology—An international organization that publishes a newsletter and lists various graduate programs in transpersonal (holistic) psychology.

Chinook Learning Center—A learning center that features seminars and workshops designed to effect personal and global harmony. Seminars are offered on topics such as "Spiritual and Cultural Transformation" and "Ritual and Ceremony."

Esalen Institute—A human potential group that explores trends in religion, philosophy, science, and education. The group offers a variety of seminars and workshops for mind, body, and soul at its Big Sur, California, location.

Farm, The—A counter-cultural New Age community in Summertown, Tennessee. This group does humanitarian work in America and abroad through its PLENTY Project.

Findhorn—A prototype New Age community located in Scotland that offers an ongoing educational program in the principles of New Age spirituality and world service. The community emphasizes the sacredness of everyday living.

Forum, The—Founded by Werner Erhard (of Est fame), The Forum targets the business community for its human potential seminars. The group teaches that each person creates his or her own reality and that people are responsible to no one but themselves. Human beings are depicted as having limitless potential.

Global Education Associates—This group seeks to engender a planetary perspective in young people. The group conducts intensive educational programs for the general public and provides speakers and consulting services for schools, religious organizations, and community groups.

Green Party—A growing political party that seeks to challenge traditional politics by emphasizing issues such as ecology, feminism, disarmament, nonviolence, and "human-scale democracy."

Greenpeace U.S.A.—A nonprofit environmental organization with over 2.5 million supporters worldwide. The goal of the group is to engender a "planetary consciousness" in the world. They promote ocean ecology, disarmament, and the prevention of toxic pollution. They accomplish their goals by two means: educating people and legislative lobbying.

Interface—A group that sponsors activities on a variety of New Age interests including consciousness, meditation, and transpersonal psychology. They also offer body-mind classes and workshops.

Lifespring—A New Age consciousness-raising group that offers human potential seminars. Lifespring teaches that man is perfect and good just the way he is, promises enlightenment to its clients, and is similar to The Forum in its emphasis that people create their own reality.

Lucis Trust—Originally incorporated as the Lucifer Publishing Company, this group publishes and promotes the writings of New Age prophetess Alice Bailey.

Pacific Institute—A group that offers human potential seminars with an emphasis on self-actualization through visualization and affirmation. Clients include many Fortune 500 companies.

Planetary Citizens—An activist group committed to engendering a "planetary consciousness" among New Age groups and the general public. The group seeks to influence world leaders in this direction.

Self-Realization Fellowship—This group provides home-study lessons that focus on Kriya Yoga meditation techniques and the teachings of the late Paramahansa Yogananda. The group seeks to train students in the harmonious development of body, mind, and soul.

Sierra Club, The—A nonprofit group that promotes conservation of the natural environment by attempting to influence public policy decisions. Volunteer activists associated with the group involve themselves in letter-writing campaigns and political lobbying. Not all involved are necessarily New Agers.

Sirius Community—A community that sponsors a full week of workshops in a spiritual living environment. This group incorporates meditation and dance into their daily routine. The group also offers day and weekend programs on topics such as holistic health and mythology.

Tara Center—New Age organization headed by writer/lecturer Benjamin Creme. With the Tara Center as his platform, Creme often speaks on the emerging New Age and its social, political, and economical order.

Theosophical Society—A group that promotes the ideas of Helena Petrovna Blavatsky and Annie Besant. The goals of the group are to (1) form a universal brotherhood; (2) do comparative study of world religions, science, and philosophy; and (3) explore the psychic and spiritual powers latent in man.

Unity-in-Diversity Counsel—A New Age "metanetwork" of over 100 networks and groups. The Counsel promotes global cooperation and interdependence on a worldwide scale.

Windstar Foundation—A group founded by John Denver that promotes "global awareness" and "a sustainable future." They also sponsor programs in ecology, conflict-resolution, and citizen diplomacy.

New Age Books

Aquarian Conspiracy, The—by Marilyn Ferguson (Los Angeles: J.P. Tarcher, Inc., 1980). This book explores New Age activities and inroads into our culture and suggests that these changes signal a transformation so radical that it may lead to an entirely new phase in evolution.

Aquarian Gospel of Jesus the Christ, The—by Levi (Santa Monica, Calif.: DeVorss & Co., 1907). A book that promotes the idea that all things are God and all things are one. Also argues that Jesus came not to free people from their sins but to display and prove the possibilities of man.

Coming of the Cosmic Christ, The—by Matthew Fox (New York: Harper and Row, 1988). A book espousing "Creation Spirituality," a system of thought characterized by mysticism, feminism, panentheism, and environmentalism. The Cosmic Christ is "the pattern that connects" or joins heaven with earth and divinity with humanity.

Earth at Omega—by Donald Keys (New York: Branden Press, 1982). Keys argues that humanity is on the verge of a giant evolutionary step. This evolutionary step will lead to a global civilization. Leading this "passage to planetization" is the "New Consciousness" movement represented by

New Age groups such as Findhorn, Esalen, and the Association for Humanistic Psychology.

Externalisation of the Hierarchy, The—by Alice Bailey (New York: Lucis Publishing Co., 1957). A book that focuses on the work and activities of the Spiritual Hierarchy, a group of exalted and ascended masters who guide the spiritual destiny of man. These ascended masters are involved in the outworking of "the Plan."

Gaia—by James E. Lovelock (New York: Oxford University Press, 1979). "Gaia" is an ancient Greek name for goddess of the earth. Lovelock's hypothesis is that the earth and all life on the earth is a single self-supporting organism.

Heart of Philosophy, The—by Jacob Needleman (New York: Bantam, 1984). Needleman is considered a pioneer in the development of a "new consciousness." Needleman argues in this book for the need for the esoteric and the mystical in Christianity.

Key to Theosophy, The—by Helena Petrovna Blavatsky (Pasadena, Calif.: Theosophical University Press, 1972). Focuses on the goals of Theosophy, which are to (1) form a universal brotherhood; (2) do comparative study of world religions, science, and philosophy; and (3) explore the psychic and spiritual powers latent in man.

Networking—by Jessica Lipnack and Jeffrey Stamps (New York: Doubleday, 1982). This book is essentially a catalogue of about 1,500 diverse New Age networks. The authors point out that networks are autonomous, hence non-conspiratorial, but often benefit from working together because of their common values and visions.

New Age Politics—by Mark Satin (New York: Delta Books, 1979). Satin believes that "the new politics" will arise out of diverse movements which can unite to work toward a common goal. These groups include the environmental, feminist, and human potential groups. The New Age political agenda is holistically oriented.

Passages About Earth: An Exploration of the New Planetary Culture—by William Irwin Thompson (New York: Harper and Row, 1973). Thompson's book traces the emergence of the New Age world view. He believes our world is now moving from "civilization" to "planetization."

Reappearance of Christ and the Masters of Wisdom, The—by Benjamin Creme (North Hollywood, Calif.: Tara Center, 1980). Creme believes the second coming of Christ has occurred in the person of "Lord Maitreya." Creme's Tara Center financed full-page ads in twenty newspapers announcing the arrival of the New Age Christ.

Reflections on the Christ—by David Spangler (Forres, Scotland: Findhorn Publications, 1981). As New Agers often do, Spangler draws a distinction between Jesus and the Christ. Jesus was a mere human who acted as a bodily vehicle for the Cosmic Christ.

Revelation: The Birth of a New Age—by David Spangler (Middleton: The Lorian Press, 1976). Spangler claims to have received many revelations from an entity named "John." These revelations, covering a diversity of New Age themes, are recorded in the book.

Tao of Physics, The—by Fritjof Capra (New York: Bantam, 1984). A book that explores the parallels between quantum physics and Eastern mysticism.

Transformations of Man, The—by Lewis Mumford (New York: Harper, 1970). The book argues that every transformation human society undergoes rests on a shift in world views. A planetary culture is presently emerging, says Mumford, that will transcend national boundaries and religious differences.

Turning Point, The—by Fritjof Capra (New York: Simon and Schuster, 1982). Building on his earlier book, *The Tao of Physics*, Capra continues to show the parallels between modern physics and Eastern mysticism. Both physics and mysticism, says Capra, show the interrelatedness of all things in the universe.

Vision of the Aquarian Age, A—by George Trevelyan (Walpole, N.H.: Stillpoint Publishing, 1984). Trevelyan focuses on the "emerging spiritual world view." He believes that all reality is sacred and divine.

New Age Magazines and Journals

Body, Mind & Spirit—A bimonthly magazine covering the New Age as well as ecological and metaphysical topics.

The magazine seeks to assist people in the self-transformation process to improve body, mind, and spirit.

EastWest—A monthly magazine that focuses on holistic health, quality of life, and alternatives to modern medicine.

Journal of Humanistic Psychology—A quarterly journal that explores personal growth, human potential, and holistic health.

New Age Journal—A bimonthly magazine emphasizing personal fulfillment and social change. This journal functions as a national mouthpiece for many New Age leaders and writers.

New Age Living—Published annually by *New Age Journal*. It contains a catalog of various New Age groups and their services.

New Realities—A bimonthly magazine that promotes oneness of self, mind, and body.

Revision—A scholarly New Age journal.

World Goodwill Newsletter—A publication promoting Alice Bailey-oriented ideas. Contains information on world affairs and programs of World Goodwill.

Yoga Journal—Published bimonthly by the California Yoga Teachers Association. Covers all aspects of yoga and holistic health.

A New Age Glossary

Often in dialogue with those involved with New Age ideas, one encounters a veritable semantic jungle. It is difficult enough to pinpoint and pin down elusive New Age concepts and occultic ideas without being hampered by confused meanings and undefined terms. This is by no means an exhaustive analysis of New Age terminology, but experience has shown that a proper understanding of terms can save a great deal of time when confronting New Agers with the claims of the gospel of Christ.

Age of Aquarius—Astrologers believe that evolution goes through cycles corresponding to the signs of the zodiac, each lasting from 2,000 to 2,400 years. New Age advocates say we are now moving from the cycle associated with Pisces into the one associated with Aquarius. The Aquarian Age will supposedly be characterized by a heightened degree of spiritual or cosmic consciousness.

Agent—A person sending a telepathic message.

Akashic Record—Imperishable records of every person's

every word, thought or act inscribed in the earth or spirit realms.

Alpha—The physical body.

Animism—The belief that inanimate things (such as plants) possess a soul or spirit. New Age advocates see animism as a way of rededicating the earth.

Anthroposophy—An esoteric cult founded by German mystic Rudolf Steiner. The term literally means "wisdom of man." It teaches that we possess the truth within ourselves. The system of thought is occultic and spiritistic.

Ascended Masters—Refers to those who have supposedly reached the highest level of spiritual consciousness and have become guides of the spiritual evolution of mankind.

Ascension of Christ—This is reinterpreted in a mystical way to refer to the rise of the "Christ-consciousness" in mankind. It describes the awareness that man is divine.

Astral Body—A spiritual body capable of projection from the physical body. The astral body survives death.

Astral Flight—Soul travel occurring particularly during sleep or deep meditation.

Attunement—A New Age counterpart to prayer. Also referred to as at-one-ment, the term relates primarily to the New Age idea that complete oneness with God can be experienced by human beings.

Aura—Radiated glow or halo surrounding living beings.

Automatic Writing—Writing produced without conscious thought of a living person; written message given through a spirit guide with a pencil or typewriter.

Avatar—A person who "descends" into human form from above as a manifestation of divinity and who reveals divine truth to people. Such a one has supposedly progressed beyond the need to be reincarnated in another body (i.e., there is no further "bad karma" to work off).

Bhagavad Gita—Hindu sacred scripture.

Blood of Christ—This is understood by some New Agers to refer to the "life-energy" of the Cosmic Christ. This "blood" supposedly flowed from the cross into the etheric (or spiritual) realms of the earth. From these realms, the Christ seeks to guide the spiritual evolution of mankind.

Bodhisattva—A being who has supposedly earned the right to enter into Nirvana or into illumination, but instead voluntarily turns back from that state in order to aid humanity in attaining the same goal. The Christ is said to be a Bodhisattva.

Buddha—"The Enlightened One." An avatar or messenger.

Channeling—A New Age form of mediumship or spiritism. The channeler yields control of his/her perceptual and cognitive capacities to a spiritual entity with the intent of receiving paranormal information.

Chinook Learning Community—A New Age educational community located in the Pacific Northwest. This group sponsors both long- and short-term educational programs on personal and social transformation, New Age spirituality, and how to live with an ecological perspective.

Clairaudience—Ability to hear mentally without using the ears.

Clairvoyance—Ability to see mentally without using the eyes, beyond ordinary time and space limits; also called "Second Sight."

Consciousness Revolution—New Age advocates call for a "consciousness revolution" a new way of looking at and experiencing life. The primary focus of the new consciousness is *oneness* with God, all mankind, the earth, and with the entire universe.

Control—The Spirit that sends messages through a medium in trance.

Cosmic Christ—In esoteric schools of thought, the Christ is considered to be a universal spirit or a cosmic force. The primary goal of this impersonal spirit or force is to guide the spiritual evolution of mankind.

Cosmic Consciousness—A spiritual and mystical perception that all in the universe is "one." To attain cosmic consciousness is to see the universe as God and God as the universe.

Cosmic Humanism—In contrast to normative humanism that sees man as the measure of all things, cosmic humanism sees man as having virtually unlimited potential because of his inner divinity.

Crystals—New Age advocates believe that crystals contain incredible healing and energizing powers. Crystals are often touted as being able to restore the "flow of energy" in the human body.

Deja Vu—The feeling of having already experienced an event or place that is being encountered for the very first time.

Discarnate—The soul or personality of a living creature who has died.

Dowser—A sensitive who uses a forked stick that points to hidden water, oil, buried money, lost articles, or people.

Earth Logos—Some New Age advocates believe that the Earth Logos is a great spiritual being who is the ensouling life of planet earth. The earth is considered a physical manifestation (or body) of this spiritual intelligence.

Ectoplasm—A white filmy substance pouring from a medium's bodily openings, supposedly denoting the presence of a disembodied spirit.

Esalen Institute—A "growth center" that offers a wide variety of workshops for mind, body, and spirit. It is located in Big Sur, California.

Esoteric—A word used to describe knowledge that is possessed or understood only by a few.

Esoteric Christianity—A mystical form of Christianity that sees its "core truth" as identical to the "core truth" of every other religion (i.e., man is divine). This form of Christianity is at home with Aldous Huxley's "perennial philosophy." (See: Perennial Philosophy.)

ESP—Extrasensory perception encompassing paranormal abilities such as telepathy, precognition, and clairvoyance.

ESP Cards—A pack of twenty-five cards bearing five symbols, including stars, squares, circles, crosses, and waves.

Exoteric Christianity—A form of Christianity identified with historic or orthodox Christianity that New Agers would describe as being devoid of all spiritual authenticity.

Fall of Man—Refers to the fall of man's consciousness. A fallen consciousness is one that recognizes the existence of only the material realm. The Christ is believed to have "redeemed" man in the sense that he enabled man to perceive the spiritual world behind the material world.

Findhorn Community—A legendary New Age community located in the North of Scotland. This group offers an ongoing educational program in the principles of New Age spirituality.

Gaia—A Greek name for the goddess of the earth. It also refers to a scientific hypothesis formulated by James Lovelock whereby all living matter on the earth is believed to be a single living organism. In such a scheme, humanity is considered the nervous system of the living earth.

Globalism—A modern-day term referring to the need for a transformation from the present nation-state divisions into a one-world community.

Gnosticism—A tradition going back to the second century which holds that salvation comes through intuitive "gnosis" or knowledge of one's supposed divinity.

God—A being who has "many faces." He (it) is considered a radically immanent being who is often referred to as a "universal consciousness," "universal life," or "universal energy." The New Age god is more or less an impersonal force that pervades the universe.

Graphology—Character analysis and foretelling based on handwriting.

Great Invocation, The—A New Age prayer that has been translated into over eighty languages. The purpose of this prayer is to invoke the presence of the Cosmic Christ on earth, thus leading to the oneness and brotherhood of all mankind.

Group Guru—A slang New Age term referring to the idea that the Cosmic Christ is incarnate in all of humanity. All mankind is seen as a single "guru."

Guru—Teacher or master.

Harmonic Convergence—The assembly of New Age meditators gathered at the same propitious astrological time in different locations to usher in peace on earth and one-world government.

Holism—The theory that all reality is organically one. Everything in the universe is viewed as interrelated and interdependent.

Holistic Health—Holistic health sees the body as an interrelated organism. Its goal is to treat the whole person (body, mind, and spirit) as opposed to merely treating a particular sickness.

Hologram—A three-dimensional projection resulting from the interaction of laser beams. Scientists have discovered that the image of an entire hologram can be reproduced from any one of its many component parts. New Agers use this to illustrate the oneness of all reality.

Human Potential Movement—A movement with roots in humanistic psychology that stresses man's essential goodness and unlimited potential.

Initiation—This occult term is generally used in reference to the expansion or transformation of a person's consciousness. An "initiate" is one whose consciousness has been transformed so that he now perceives inner realities. There are varying "degrees" of initiation (i.e., "first-degree initiates," "second-degree initiates," etc.).

Inner Self/Higher Self—Refers to the inner divine nature possessed by human beings. All people are said to possess an inner self, though not all are aware of it.

Interdependence/Interconnectedness—These words are used by New Agers to describe the oneness and essential unity of everything in the universe. All of reality is viewed as interdependent and interconnected.

Jesus—An avatar who attained a high level of attunement to the Cosmic Christ. This enabled him to become a bodily vehicle for the Christ for a period of three years. (See: Avatar)

Kabala—Hebrew mystery lore based on mystical interpretation of the Bible; magical, occult practices stemming largely from the Middle Ages.

Karma—Refers to the "debt" accumulated against a soul as a result of good or bad actions committed during one's life (or lives). If one accumulates good karma, he will supposedly be reincarnated in a desirable state. If one accumulates bad karma, he will be reincarnated in a less desirable state.

Kirlian Photography—A photographic process that measures living auras.

Kundalini—The elemental energy of the human body which, like a serpent, rests coiled at the base of the spine.

Levitation—Raising of objects or people off the ground without using physical energy.

Lucis Trust—Originally incorporated as the Lucifer Publishing Company, the Lucis Trust oversees the Lucis Publishing Company, World Goodwill, and Arcane School. Lucis Trust owns all the copyrights of the Alice Bailey books.

Magic Circle—Ring drawn by occultists to protect them from the spirits and demons they call up by incantations and rituals.

Maitreya—The name has its roots in a legendary Buddha figure. Some New Age advocates believe that the "second coming of Christ" occurred in 1977 in the person of Maitreya.

Mandala—A design, usually concentric, that focuses attention to a single point.

Mantra—A word or phrase that is to be chanted repetitively in an effort to empty the mind and attain "cosmic consciousness" (oneness with God and the universe).

Mass Incarnation—An incarnation of the Christ in all of humanity. New Age advocates say that this incarnation is presently taking place on a planetary scale, and is not unlike the incarnation of the Cosmic Christ in the body of Jesus 2,000 years ago.

Medium—A psychic or sensitive living person whose body is used as a vehicle for communicating with spirits.

Metaphysics—The science of the supernatural.

Monism—A metaphysical theory that sees all of reality as a unified whole. Everything in the universe is seen as being made of the same stuff.

Network—An informal, decentralized organization created by like-minded individuals who are interested in addressing specific problems and offering possible solutions. All of this takes place outside of conventional institutions.

New Age Movement—A loose organization of people, many of them "Yuppies," who believe the world has entered the Aquarian Age when peace on earth and one-world government will rule. They see themselves as advanced in consciousness, rejecting Judeo-Christian values and the Bible in favor of Oriental philosophies and religion. Among them may be found environmentalists, nuclear-freeze proponents, Marxist-socialist utopians, mind-control advocates, ESP cultists, spiritists, witchcraft practitioners, and others using magical rites.

Nirvana—Liberation from earthly things; paradise.

Numerology—The analysis of hidden or prophetic meanings of numbers.

Occultism—Belief in supernational forces and beings.

Om—A word symbolizing Brahma, the Creator God.

One Worlders—Those who advocate the abolition of nations, working to hand over power to a single-world government similar in structure to the present United Nations; offshoots of the United World Federalists founded in the 1930s.

Ouiji Board—Game board containing all the letters of the alphabet plus numbers from 0 to 9 and "Yes/No." A sliding pointer (planchette) spells out words in answer to questions asked by players.

Out-of-Body Experience—Leaving the physical body while at rest, asleep, near death, or temporarily dead.

Pantheism—Doctrine that identifies God with the whole universe, every particle, tree, table, animal, and person being part of Him.

Paradigm Shift—Refers to a shift in world views. The so-called "new paradigm" (new *model* or *form*) is pantheistic (all is God) and monistic (all is one).

Paranormal—Beyond or above normal human powers or senses.

Parapsychology—Study of psychic phenomena using scientific methods.

Pendulum—Heavy object on a string, used for dowsing or fortune telling.

Pentagram—Five-pointed star used in magical ceremonies. A satanic symbol.

Percipient—Person who receives telepathic messages.

Perennial Philosophy—A term coined by Aldous Huxley that sees all religious truth or experience as one and the same. This philosophy proposes that even though the externals of the various religions may differ, the essence or core truth is the same in each.

Plan, The—A phrase that occurs often in the writings of Alice Bailey. It refers to specific preparations in the world for a New Age and a New Age Christ. These preparations are carried out by the "Masters of the Hierarchy," a group of exalted beings who supposedly guide the spiritual evolution of people on earth. Though this teaching of the Plan does actually exist, the term has been sensationalized by some Christian writers. These writers have mistakenly hypothesized that New Agers are completely unified in a "behind-the-scenes manipulation" of world events in order to conquer the world for its true god, Lucifer.

Planetary Citizens—A New Age activist group committed to engendering a "planetary consciousness" among both New Agers and the general public.

Planetization—New Age advocates believe that the various threats facing the human race require a global solution. This solution is "planetization." The word refers to the unifying of the world into a corporate brotherhood.

Poltergeist—German word for a noisy, mischievous, destructive spirit (a demon).

Precognition—Advance knowledge of future events.

PSI—Term used in place of psychic or paraphysical; ESP.

Psychic Birth—A quickening of spiritual or cosmic consciousness and power. This new consciousness is one that recognizes oneness with God and the universe. Psychic birth is an occult counterpart to the Christian new birth.

Psychic Energy—Extrasensory energy that enables people to do miracles.

Psychic Healer—A person who cures mental or physical illness from the cosmic energy emanating through the healer's hands.

Psychoanalysis—Tracing mental and physical ills back to hurtful childhood experiences; based on Sigmund Freud's theories.

Psychometry—Reading information from an object about events involving the person who owns it, usually by handling it.

Psychotechnologies—Refers to the various approaches or systems aimed at deliberately altering one's consciousness.

Reincarnation—Refers to the cyclical evolution of a person's soul as it repeatedly passes from one body to another at death. This process continues until the soul reaches a state of perfection.

Retrocognition—Knowledge of past events learned paranormally.

Right Brain Learning—The right hemisphere of the brain is believed to be the center of intuitive and creative thought (as opposed to the rational nature of the left hemisphere). New Agers have seized on this as a justification to bring "right brain learning techniques" into the classroom. These techniques include meditation, yoga, and guided imagery.

Seance—A gathering of people seeking communication with deceased loved ones or famous historical figures through a medium.

Second Coming of Christ—Understood by some as the coming of the Cosmic Christ in all of humanity, related to the New age concept of the "mass incarnation." The Second Coming is supposedly now occurring in the hearts and minds of people all over the earth. Others associate it specifically with the appearance of Maitreya as the avatar of this age.

Self-realization—New Agers use this as a synonym for God-realization. It refers to a personal recognition of one's divinity.

Sensitive—A person who frequently demonstrates extrasensory gifts such as clairvoyance, telepathy, or precognition.

Shaman—A medicine man or witch doctor.

Solar Logos—Believed by some to be a mighty spiritual being who is the ensouling life of the solar system. The material solar system is simply a physical manifestation (or body) of this living intelligence.

Spirit Control—A disembodied spirit who relays messages from dead people to the living through a trance medium.

Spirit Guide—A spiritual entity who provides information of "guidance," often through a medium or channeler. The spirit provides guidance only after the channeler relinquishes his perceptual and cognitive capacities into its control.

Spiritual Hierarchy of Masters—New Age advocates believe these spiritual "masters" are highly evolved men who, having already perfected themselves, are now guiding the rest of humanity to this same end.

Spiritualist or Spiritist—Person who believes in the ability to contact departed souls through a medium.

Subject—Person used for experiments in ESP studies.

Sufism—Persian mystical religion based on Islam.

Syncretism—The attempt to combine or unify differing religious systems. New Age gurus often claim that all the world religions teach the same core truth: all people possess an inner divinity.

Synergy—A principle which states that the whole is greater than the sum of its parts.

Taoism—A Chinese religion and philosophy that sees the universe as engaged in ceaseless motion and activity. All is considered to be in continual flux. The universe is intrinsically dynamic. This continual cosmic process is called the "Tao" by the Chinese. The process is described in terms of Yin and Yang. (See: Yin/Yang.)

Tarot Cards—Deck of seventy-eight cards that supposedly reveal the secrets of man and the universe.

Telekinesis—The ability to move physical objects by force of will or mental energy alone; also called psychokinesis.

Telepathy—Communication between minds by extrasensory means.

Tetragram—A magic diagram shaped as a four-pointed star.

Theosophy—A school of thought founded by Helena P. Blavatsky. The term literally means "divine wisdom." The goals of Theosophy are to (1) form a universal brotherhood; (2) do comparative study of world religions, science, and philosophy; and, (3) investigate the psychic and spiritual powers latent in man. Theosophy is the forerunner of much New Age thought.

Third Eye—An imaginary eye in the forehead believed to be the center of psychic vision.

Trance—A mental state resembling sleep during which the conscious mind rests while the spirit entity takes over the medium's body.

Trance Channeler—The newest term for "trance medium." (See: Medium.)

Transformation—New Age advocates promote both personal and planetary transformation. *Personal* transformation involves the changes wrought in one's life by increasing Self-realization. As more and more people are personally transformed, the *planet* too will be transformed into a global brotherhood.

Trumpet Medium—A psychic or sensitive who brings forth "spirit voices" through a trumpet at seances.

UFO—Unidentified flying object; flying saucer.

Unity-in-Diversity Council—A New Age "metanetwork" of over 100 networks and groups rallying for global cooperation and interdependence.

Veda—The most ancient of the Hindu scriptures.

Visualization—Also known as "guided imagery," visualization basically refers to "mind over matter." It involves the attempt to bring about change in the material realm by the power of the mind.

Warlock—A wizard or sorcerer; a male witch.

World Goodwill—A New Age political lobby that aims to unfold "the Plan" as spelled out in the writings of Alice Bailey.

Yin/Yang—Chinese names referring to the active and passive principles of the universe. *Yin* refers to the female or [inactive] negative force; *Yang* to the male or active force. These two polar forces continually interplay with each other. The words are used to describe the constant flow of motion and change in the universe (i.e., the "Tao").

Yoga—A means of becoming united with the supreme being, or with the universal soul.

Yogi—Someone who practices yoga.

New Age Bibliography: A Recommended Reading List

Albrecht, Mark. *Reincarnation: A Christian Appraisal.* Downers Grove, Ill.: InterVarsity Press, 1982.

———. *Reincarnation: A Christian Critique of a New Age Doctrine.* Downers Grove, Ill.: InterVarsity Press, 1987.

Anglican Church of Canada. *The Book of Alternative Services of the Anglican Church of Canada.* Toronto, Ontario, Canada: Anglican Book Centre, 1985.

Bartley, W.W. *Werner Erhard: the Transformation of a Man: the Founding of EST.* New York: Clarkson N. Potter, 1978.

Blumenfeld, Samuel L. *NEA: Trojan Horse in American Education.* Boise, Idaho: Paradigm, 1984.

Bobgan, Martin and Diedre. *Hypnosis and the Christian.* Minneapolis, Minn.: Bethany House, 1984.

———. *The Psychological Way/The Spiritual Way.* Minneapolis, Minn.: Bethany Fellowship, 1979.

Brand, Paul and Philip Yancey. "A Surgeon's View of Divine Healing." *Christianity Today,* (November 25, 1983).

Breese, Dave. *Know the Marks of Cults.* Wheaton, Ill.: Victor Books, 1986.

Bube, A. "Science and Pseudoscience." *The Reformed Journal,* No. 32 (Nov. 1982).

Buell, Jon and Quentin Hyder. *Jesus: Ghost, God, or Guru.* Grand Rapids, Mich.: Zondervan/Probe, 1978.

Castaneda, C. *The Teaching of Don Juan.* Berkeley: University of California Press, 1969.

Cocciardi, Carol; Mary Cocciardi; Karen Erickson; and Linda Erickson, eds. *The Psychic Yellow Pages*. Saratoga, Calif.: Out of the Sky, 1977.

Coleman, K. "Elisabeth Kubler-Ross in the Afterworld of Entities." *New West* (July 30, 1979).

Cole-Whittaker, T. *How to Have More in a Have-Not World*. New York: Fawcett Crest, 1983.

Creme, B. *The Reappearance of the Christ and the Masters of Wisdom*. London: Tara Press, 1980.

Cumby, C. *The Hidden Dangers of the Rainbow*. Shreveport, La.: Huntington House, 1983.

Dietrich, B. "The Coming of a New Age." *Seattle Times* (Jan. 18, 1987).

Enroth, Ronald, ed. *A Guide to Cults and New Religions*. Downers Grove, Ill.: InterVarsity Press, 1983.

———. *The Lure of the Cults and New Religions*. Downers Grove, Ill.: InterVarsity Press, 1987.

Ferguson, M. *The Aquarian Conspiracy*. Los Angeles: J.P. Tarcher, 1980.

Flew, Anthony. "Miracles." *The Encyclopedia of Philosophy*, Paul Edwards ed., vol. 5. New York: Macmillan, 1967.

Fuller, John. *Arigo: Surgeon of the Rusty Knife*. New York: Thomas Crowell Co, 1974.

Gabler, Mel and Norma. *What Are They Teaching Our Children?* Wheaton, Ill.: Victor Books, 1985.

Geisler, Norman and J. Yutaka Amano. *The Reincarnation Sensation*. Wheaton, Ill.: Tyndale, 1986.

Geisler, Norman and J. Kerby Anderson. *Origin Science*. Grand Rapids, Mich.: Baker, 1987.

Goodspead, E. *Famous "Biblical" Hoaxes*. Grand Rapids, Mich.: Baker Book House, 1956.

Grenier, Richard. *The Ghandi Nobody Knows*. Nashville, Tenn.: Nelson, 1983.

Groothuis, Douglas R. *Unmasking the New Age*. Downers Grove, Ill.: InterVarsity Press, 1986.

———. *Confronting the New Age*. Downers Grove, Ill.: InterVarsity Press, 1988.

Hanley, J. *The Lifespring Family News*, vol. 1.

Head, Joseph, and S.L. Cranston. *Reincarnation: The Phoenix Fire Mystery*. New York: Warner, 1977.

Heinberg, Richard. *Memories and Visions of Paradise*. Loveland, Co.: Emissaries of Divine Light, 1985.

Hexham, Irving and Karla Poewe. *Understanding Cults and New Religions*. Grand Rapids, Mich.: Eerdmans, 1986.

Hicks, D. and D. Lewis. *The Todd Phenomenon*. Harrison, Ark.: New Leaf Press, 1979.

Hoyt, Karen, ed. *The Cult Explosion*. Irvine, Calif.: Harvest House, 1987.

Hunt, Dave. *Peace, Prosperity and the Coming Holocaust*. Eugene, Ore.: Harvest House, 1983.

Hunt, Dave, and T.A. McMahon. *The Seduction of Christianity*. Eugene, Ore.: Harvest House, 1985.

Hurkos, Peter. *Psychic*. Indianapolis: Bobbs-Merrill, 1961.

Ingham, Michael. *Rites For a New Age: Understanding the Book of Alternative Services*. Toronto, Ontario, Canada: The Anglican Book Centre, 1986.

Jastrow, Robert. *God and the Astronomers*. New York: Norton, 1978.

Kilpatrick, K. *The Emperor's New Clothes*. Westchester, Ill.: Crossway Books, 1985.

Knight, J. *I Am Ramtha*. Portland, Ore.: Beyond Words Publishing, 1986.

Koch, Kurt. *Christian Counseling and Occultism*. Grand Rapids, Mich.: Kregel, 1972.

———. *Demonology, Past and Present*. Grand Rapids, Mich.: Kregel, 1973.

———. *Occult Bondage and Deliverance*. Grand Rapids, Mich.: Kregel, 1976.

Kole, Andre, and Al Janssen. *Miracles or Magic?* Eugene, Ore.: Harvest House, 1984.

Korem, Danny and Paul Meier. *The Fakers*. Grand Rapids, Mich.: Baker, 1980.

LeShan, Lawrence. *The Medium, the Mystic and the Physicist*. New York: Random House, Ballantine Books, 1975.

Lewis, C.S. *The Screwtape Letters*. Old Tappan, N.J.: Revell, 1976.

Maharaj, Rabi. *Escape Into the Light*. Eugene, Ore.: Harvest House, 1984.

Maharishi, Mahesh Yogi. *Meditations of Maharishi Mahesh Yogi*. New York: Bantam Books, 1968.

Marin, P. "The New Narcissism." *Harper's* (Oct. 1975).

Matrisciana, Caryl. *Gods of the New Age*. Eugene, Ore.: Harvest House, 1985.

Matzat, Don. *Inner Healing*. Eugene, Ore.: Harvest House, 1987.

Michaelsen, Johanna. *The Beautiful Side of Evil*. Eugene, Ore.: Harvest House, 1982.

Miller, Roberta DeLong. *Psychic Massage*. New York: Harper and Row, Harper Colophon Books, 1975.

Moody, Raymond A. *Life After Life*. New York: Bantam, 1975.

Morey, Robert A. *Horoscopes and the Christian*. Minneapolis, Minn.: Bethany House, 1981.

———. *Reincarnation and Christianity*. Minneapolis, Minn.: Bethany House, 1980.

Moss, Thelma. *The Probability of the Impossible*. New York: New American Library, 1975.

Neibuhr, R. *Christian Realism and World Problems*. New York: Scribner, 1953.

Nolen, William A. *Healing: A Doctor in Search of a Miracle*. New York: Random House, 1974.

North, Gary. *Unholy Spirits; Occultism and New Age Humanism*. Tyler, Tex.: Dominion Press, 1986.

Pement, Eric. *The 1988 Directory of Cult Research Organizations*. Chicago, Ill.: Cornerstone Press, 1988.

Playfair, Guy Lyon. *The Unknown Power*. New York: Pocket Books, 1975.

Puharich, Andrijah. *Beyond Death's Door*. Nashville, Tenn.: Nelson, 1978.

Rajneesh. *Come Follow Me: 2*. Poona, India: Rajneesh Foundation, 1977.

Randi, James. *Flim-Flam*. Buffalo: Prometheus, 1982.

Raschke, Carl A. *The Interruption of Eternity: Modern Gnosticism and the Origins of the New Religious Consciousness*. Chicago, Ill.: Nelson-Hall, 1980.

Reisser, Paul C., Teri K. Reisser, and John Weldon. *The Holistic Healers.* Downers Grove, Ill.: InterVarsity Press, 1983.

————. *New Age Medicine.* Downers Grove, Ill.: InterVarsity Press, 1987.

Russell, P. *The Global Brain.* Los Angeles, Calif.: J.P. Tarcher, 1983.

Schlafly, Phyllis, ed. *Child Abuse in the Classroom.* Westchester, Ill.: Crossway, 1984.

Sire, James. *Scripture Twisting.* Downers Grove, Ill.: InterVarsity Press, 1980.

————. *The Universe Next Door*, 2nd ed. Downers Grove, Ill.: InterVarsity Press, 1988.

Snyder, John. *Reincarnation vs. Resurrection.* Chicago, Ill.: Moody, 1984.

Spangler, D. *Explorations.* Scotland: Findhorn, 1980.

"Spiritism: the Medium and the Message." *Spiritual Counterfeits Project Journal*, vol. 7, no. 1, 1987.

Spiritual Fitness in Business Newsletter. Richardson, Tex.: Probe Ministries.

Stearn, J. *The Power of Alpha-thinking: Miracle of the Mind.* New York: William Morrow, 1976.

Stevenson, Ian. *Twenty Cases Suggestive of Reincarnation.* New York: American Society for Physical Research, 1966.

Stott, John. *The Authentic Jesus.* Downers Grove, Ill.: InterVarsity Press.

Talbot, M. *Mysticism and the New Physics.* New York: Bantam Books, 1981.

Thompson, W. *From Nations to Emanation.* Scotland: Findhorn, 1982.

Van Buskirk, Michael. *Astrology: Revival in the Cosmic Garden.* Santa Ana, Calif.: Christian Apologetics: Research and Information Service.

Vitz, Paul C. *Censorship.* Ann Arbor, Mich.: Servant, 1986.

————. *Psychology as Religion.* Grand Rapids, Mich.: Eerdmans, 1977.

Webb, J. *The Occult Establishment.* LaSalle, Ill.: Open Court Publishing, 1976.

Weldon, John and James Bjornstad. *Playing With Fire.* Chicago:Moody, 1984.

Wimber, John, and Kevin Springer. *Power Evangelism.* San Francisco: Harper and Row, 1986.

————. *Power Healing.* San Francisco: Harper and Row, 1987.